architecture in transition

architecture

Constantinos A. Doxiadis

in transition

New York
Oxford University Press
1963

First published 1963

Printed in Great Britain

to the architects who are young in heart

acknowledgements

Particular acknowledgements are due to my collaborators for help in making this book possible: Miss S. Zarambouka, for putting the illustrations in their final form; Mr. G. Drachman, for checking the English; Mrs. J. Zachariou and Miss P. Gregoriadis, whose skilled typing gave concrete form to these ideas; and Mr. N. Avronidakis, for the overall supervision of this work.

contents

illustrations

preface

FOR TWENTY-EIGHT YEARS now I have been expressing my views on architecture in lectures and articles, as well as in reports of all kinds. It was in 1960 that I was given the honour of delivering the annual discourse of the Royal Institute of British Architects (R.I.B.A.) under the title 'Architecture in Evolution'. During the same year I had the opportunity of speaking on various occasions to the architects and planners of the United States, Norway and Sweden, Pakistan, Ghana, Egypt and Greece.

In some of these lectures I spoke of the dilemma of the architect in our time; in others, although my subject concerned the problems of physical plans and human settlements, and my audiences included experienced architects and students, administrators and artists, economists and engineers, sociologists and geographers, I was always asked questions about architecture and the problems that architecture is facing today.

That is why I decided to publish this book on *Architecture in Transition* even before the book I really wanted to print first, that on *Ekistics*. This book attempts to provide a systematic answer to the questions which have been asked by my audiences, especially during the last few years of my lectures. While basing it principally on my discourse to the R.I.B.A., I have also expanded my treatment of a few of the questions with which it deals, and added several notions which I feel are indispensable to a general understanding of the subject as I see it.

B   17

This book is intended to stand side by side with my next books, the one on ekistics, since it is there that I present the framework of ideas which is necessary for a better understanding of the problems of architecture today, and that on ecumenopolis, since it is there that I present the physical framework of the architecture which is now created. *Architecture in Transition* is a book with which many may disagree. It is not a textbook but the statement of a creed, not a collection of statistics but one man's personal point of view. Any value it may have lies simply in this: that it is the product of years of travel, years of first-hand observation, years of thinking and talking. As such, it is written 'out of my life', and as such it is dedicated to all those architects, the young in heart, who are today asking themselves difficult questions about their role and about their road into the future.

1   architectural confusion

THE URBAN NIGHTMARE

I CAN FIND no better way to describe our cities than as an urban nightmare. If we want to speak about architecture we cannot think merely of buildings isolated in the countryside; such buildings are seldom erected nowadays, but even when they do occur they are gradually taken over by the expanding cities. In any case, to think of isolated buildings is really to evade the main question related to architecture, for architecture does in fact lead towards the formation of cities.

It does not matter whether we look at our cities from the air when we see their irrational plan, from a car on a highway or a congested street, as pedestrians on a busy sidewalk or from the inside or outside of a block of buildings; we always have the same impression of living in a nightmare.

With very few exceptions, this is true of all cities. It is true of practically everything that is being built today. But it is also true of the cities of the past, most of which, even if they were once satisfactory, have now been turned into hybrids where the old shell has to serve new needs, and where the quiet city of the past, built for human beings, has been taken over by machines and cars. I think that Venice is a remarkable exception, and it is not a coincidence that Venice has no cars and has not expanded to any important degree from the moment at which it took a certain architectural form. Venice is a city of the past preserved down to our days. It is not a confused city—and that is why we like it.

I know of no city built in our epoch of which we can be proud, and certainly no city built in the past and inhabited according to our contemporary way of living with which we can be happy. If there are still parts of cities which we enjoy visiting, they are those parts which are no longer inhabited, such as the archaeological sites, or those sections not taken over by the new way of living. The advent of motor-boats, for example, has not yet been able to change the structure of the city of Venice; fortunately, nobody has so far thought of widening its canals to allow for more motor-boat traffic, though this is no more absurd than allowing a proliferation of cars to force us to a last-minute readjustment of our major cities and even minor towns by road widening.

To live in almost any of our cities today is to live in a nightmare, an urban nightmare symbolic of so many of the problems of our epoch, for it is in the urban areas that these problems take their most obvious outward expression.

THE BIG QUESTIONS

Living in cities does not help us clear our minds about architecture. What is especially bad for us architects, who are supposed to be the leaders in the field of architectural creation, is that our role, whether as laymen or experts, is confused in many ways. So confused is it that big questions and big dilemmas are constantly being created.

Is the architect a designer of buildings? We must really examine both parts of this question, buildings and designers.

Can an architect be limited to buildings? And how about the cities? Even if we create the proper buildings, are we to leave it to somebody else to provide for their synthesis within the city, within the urban area? Are we to leave this to the traffic engineer or to the town planner? Then, what kind of town planner, a town planner who is an architect or not? I think that we must honestly admit that we have not answered this question. We do not know whether the architect is supposed to create buildings or neighbourhoods or cities.

We also spoke of designers. Are the architects really the designers of buildings? Are they entitled to remain designers or planners? Who, then, is going to create the buildings? How far are the architects entitled to limit themselves to designing, and to blame the builders, the clients or society at large for not following their designs?

Can the design be an end in itself, and can the architect be justified in limiting himself to design, instead of proceeding to the actual building or construction? I don't believe that we have managed to answer even this big query in our epoch.

Our generation is luckier than the last one in this respect: while the last one was represented by narrow-minded architects who thought themselves only designers of academic styles, we of the present generation have witnessed a revolution started by men like Le Corbusier, Gropius and Mies van der Rohe, as a result of which architects are no longer supposed to be designers of academic styles. They have remained designers none the less, and most of the schools are in fact no more than schools of architectural design, whose purpose is to create new styles.

But we have not managed to become builders. Most architects would consider themselves insulted if they were called on to participate in an effort to build instead of designing and supervising others, and would even rebel at the suggestion that they might join an industrial firm which produced architectural elements.

To be frank, we have to state clearly that as architects we are confused, because we have defined neither the content and size of our subject nor our own role in dealing with it.

THE MASTER BUILDER'S LIFE

Personally I often feel like an itinerant master builder of the past, travelling around the world and offering my services. But I do not trudge the roads with my tools on my back; on the contrary, I use the aeroplane to make my long flights all over the world. On these flights I sometimes wake up in the middle of the night and find myself in a darkened circus in the heart of a city, with bent people hurrying in different directions in the dark all around me.

I look down one street and see a building illuminated for a few moments before the darkness blots it out again, only to lift over a different street, another illuminated spot, and then another and another. Sometimes it is a skyscraper that I see, or in the opposite direction a spherical house, or maybe in the far distance a whole radiant city. At other times it may be geodetic domes, prefabricated houses or a series of shells. I see monumental architecture, monuments of the past and monuments of the present: now the Acropolis, the Gothic cathedrals, the Taj Mahal, the squares of Florence; and now the sprawling nomadic suburbs of the American, the Canadian or the Australian city. Looming over all is the city of motor-cars; houses, factories and buildings of all kinds, highways crossing the cities, but, above all, cars, cars, cars; cars driving around in the dark and passing through the architecture of the past and the present.

There I stand, frightened as a child lost in the dark, wondering which road I should take, which way I must go. And then I try to find my way, to avoid the nightmare, to face my dilemma as an architect by using the experience I have gained as an itinerant master builder.

I realize then that our problem is a problem of confusion. One generation back we tried to break our bonds with the past. We did indeed break the bonds but only of architectural design and now we are confused about our future. One generation back we had to break the shackles of academism and free ourselves to create modern architecture. We have done it, but we now find ourselves living in an urban nightmare which spreads more and more and imprisons us at its centre. In confusion we look around to find out what to do with our hard-won liberty.

2   epoch of transition

THE MAIN reason for our confusion is that we find ourselves in an epoch of transition, the general nature of which is also reflected in our architecture.

In trying to find our way in the darkness by which we are surrounded, we have to understand first where we are in space and time.

Where do we stand in space? It is too late to speak of local or national issues, too late even to speak of an Eastern or a Western world. On the other hand, it is too early, for all practical purposes, to speak about the other planets (we know so little about them as yet that it is meaningless to speculate on their particular problems). The earth is the space we are talking about; neither more nor less than our whole planet.

It is on this earth that we find ourselves living today in an age of great transition, an age where the rate of change is accelerating from one day to the next. This rate of change is the most characteristic phenomenon of our age, whether we speak of technological progress or of economic development, of population growth or of social or cultural phenomena. Our transition is a transition from old to new, from traditional to modern, from the concepts of the past to the concepts of the future, and so from the problems of the past to the problems of the future.

Architecture simply follows the general trends of its age. It is now in the process of evolution, as it has always been, but an evolution more intense and more rapid than ever before. When

23

architecture was passing from archaic to classical Greek and then from classical to Hellenistic Greek, or from Early to Late Renaissance or Baroque, the evolution was a slow one. It is no longer so today.

Evolution is now such that architectural styles are supposed to be created by everyone every day, and for the first time we are confusing architectural fashion with architectural style. It is this evolution, this transition from phase to phase, that led me to call the architecture of our times 'Architecture in Transition'.

FROM ACADEMIC TO MODERN

It is not enough to state that architecture, like everything else, is in such a phase of evolution that its most important characteristic is transition. We need to clarify this change as a change from one thing to something else.

The first and simplest definition of the change, especially for the architects and the technologically advanced groups of people, is that it is a transition from academic to modern. This is a real revolution, one which started a generation ago and has so far been successful, but which has nevertheless not yet led to a solution. Were the case otherwise, we should not be faced with such problems today.

In one way or another we have overthrown the gods of the past, but now everyone has become a god. We hear many ideas and proposals—a phenomenon which is useful up to a point. Man is everywhere trying out his new wings, but does not always reach even the lowest clouds, much less the sun. All too often our modern Icarus falls ignominiously; the streets of our cities are littered with the debris of his broken wings, the soiled and ruffled feathers.

We might perhaps say that such attempts at least give public opinion the chance of selecting from among so many proposals and ideas. But public opinion is not free, for it is the slave of its own habitat, and is bowed down under the inertia created by its own environment.

CAUGHT BETWEEN OLD AND NEW

Public opinion very often demands the traditional, but in demanding the creation of something reminiscent of the old houses, it forgets that old houses, as Lorca said, are created not by architects, but by time.

So every single one of us living in a house of the past or walking in a street of the past bears the weight of his surroundings. We are thus obliged to create the new while living in the midst of the old which is still in existence and the old which is again being imitated. 'We shape our buildings,' said Sir Winston Churchill, 'thereafter they shape us.' This is an important truth that we always forget when we speak of public opinion, and the process of the selection of the fittest. Who selects? The public. And how is the public educated in terms of architecture? Mainly by its surroundings or by popular magazines.

Let us now take an average city and study the surroundings within which the average citizen is living at a given moment X. Taking 100–120 years as the average life of the buildings in this city, anyone reaching adulthood at moment X opens his eyes every day on a city created by the four previous generations. He lives in a city which often does not correspond to its present needs. It has out-lived even its own creators, because the people who created a certain group of buildings have already been dead for more than 100 years— even assuming they started their creation at twenty and lived an average of seventy years. During his lifetime the same man will have the opportunity of adding perhaps 30 or 40 per cent to the city, but, even so, he will have worked for a city two-thirds of which he in-herited from others. In the meantime he will change his clothing several tens of times, his car several times, his industrial equipment at least three to four times; his city, however, will remain largely as he inherited it.

This fact turns the average citizen into a slave of the past in terms of architecture more than in anything else depending on him. We have therefore to deal with a public opinion which is in shackles.

Thus the average man tends to consider as right what is prevalent. This was all very well when there was no distinct change in tech-nology and ways of living, but it is no longer satisfactory now that the main characteristic of life around us is rapid change. Because of his tendency to copy what is prevalent, the average man is very con-servative. He wants to build something that looks exactly the same as what he knows and sees every day. He is therefore in favour of continuing the local traditional solutions; also, although this may seem strange, he is in favour of importing alien solutions—because he has seen them in his travels or read about them in magazines. Consequently, he is in favour of a *status quo*—his own or an imported one—and therefore opposes the evolution of existing solutions by the introduction of new ideas.

Yet the architect himself is also a slave of his own surroundings. He must indeed be a very great man to be able to detach himself from his habitat and judge it for what it is worth, keeping what is necessary but rejecting whatever can serve him no longer. Scientists liberate themselves from their surroundings by isolating only the facts which they require, and even artists can, at any stage of their lives, avoid coming under the influence of any particular style, whether contemporary or traditional. The architect is the only one who is supposed to create something better while living in, and being continuously influenced by, the work of his predecessors. He cannot help accepting many notions of the past as the natural first principles of his own creation. The architecture being created every day has to follow a difficult road loaded to breaking-point with the weight of its habitat.

This fact, namely, that both the public and the architect have to live in an environment neither created nor influenced by them, has both its good and its bad aspects. The good aspect is that the forces of inertia created by our surroundings act as a defence against changes which have not been well conceived or well thought out and which are therefore simply not the most appropriate ones. This is at times a necessary safety device. After all, even though an outright failure need not be very costly, an architect who misleads humanity will create such an investment that large numbers of people will have to suffer for many years because of the community's inability to demolish any architectural creation. In this sense it is wise to respect the architectural creation of the past and to draw from it as many useful lessons as possible.

On the other hand, however, the habitat which is there acts as a real brake since, consciously or not, people tend to consider what exists as the best guide to what should exist.

In any case, we must now recognize that humanity is trapped between old and new. If the rate of change is small then there is always time for readjustment, since the rate of change of needs is also very small, and the people are satisfied with making only such

Fig. 1.   Mies van der Rohe's conception of the skyscraper

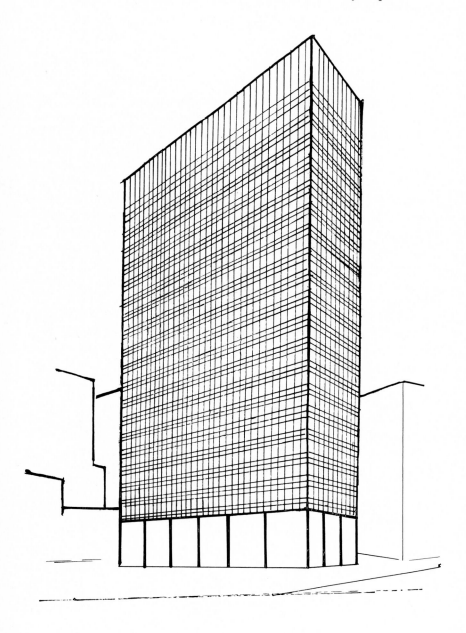

Fig. 2.   The full-shell endless house as designed by Frederick Kiesler

minor alterations to their own surroundings as can take place in the proper time. But when the rate of change of the whole society in which we are living is as great as it is today, then the slow rate of change in our habitat definitely acts as a brake on normal evolution and progress.

This is one of the big new problems of the contemporary architect. The rate of change requires him to create something which in many respects should be new, but at the same time he bears the great weight of his own habitat. Thus he is really caught between the old which cannot be demolished overnight and the new which is indispensable to the new type of life that the people have to lead.

THE MEANING OF NEW

Here we need to clarify what we mean by the new, that is, what we mean by modern. Do we mean the 'modern' of horizontal lines which was opposed at first to the 'old' of vertical lines?

Do we mean perhaps the prefabricated building or the aluminium water tank which defines the skyline of our cities? Or do we mean the spherical house, or the skyscraper, or perhaps even the full-shell endless house (Figs. 1 and 2). We have not yet answered these questions, and they remain open.

In reality we have not agreed on what is modern or new. We have very little of it anyhow, and are still surrounded by a few modern creations amid a preponderance of old ones, because economic forces and the inertia which they create do not allow us to change our habitat as easily as we change our clothes or our car.

I doubt if we really know today what is new. Thirty years ago it was easier to answer this question. Then, whatever was not old—which meant academic—whatever broke with tradition, was considered new, useful, daring and good. It was the epoch of revolution and it was necessary to encourage every effort of revolutionary importance.

But we are not entitled to think in the same way today. It is time to recognize that the revolution has not been completed, and in this respect we do need new efforts of revolutionary importance. On the other hand, however, we may no longer indiscriminately praise as right what is simply different from the old.

It is time to break the association in our minds between 'new' and 'right' and to clarify that 'new' has no meaning when it simply breaks with the past, but only when it makes a positive contribution to the future. If we look at our problems in this way we shall recognize that much of the activity taking place in factories (in the production of new materials and methods of production) and in areas of low-cost housing—no matter whether created in organized, private or governmental settlements or in a completely haphazard way—is far more important than what takes place in the ateliers of many big architects. A chemist or a production manager may in the end prove far more important to the architecture of the future than many architects.

If this fact, that even private, non-organized, low-cost housing efforts may be more important than 'big architecture', looks strange, we have only to remember that it is frequently better to let many natural forces work in their own way than to commit ourselves simply because someone has suggested the formula for a solution. In our case, if we recognize that we are in an era of transition and are confused, it is at least equally reasonable to hope that the truth may as easily come out of humble creation as out of what we call architects' architecture. How often do we fail to realize that no planning at all is better than bad planning.

FROM HANDICRAFT TO INDUSTRY

We now realize that the really new is not necessarily found on the architect's drawing-board. But let us turn to the basic changes which are occurring in architecture.

One of the most important of these is the shift of architectural creation from handicraft to industry. What was in the past a matter of local production based on the skill of the local people and the use of local materials, is now turning more and more into an activity based on materials which are produced hundreds or thousands of miles away and on constructional parts which are incorporated into buildings as whole units. Thus, where the architect was once the sole master of his creation, he is now becoming a co-ordinator of architectural creation, since he is compelled more and more to use materials and elements in the conception, production and form of which he may have played no part whatever.

At first, this trend appeared mainly in the installations of our buildings. Then it spread to some structural parts, until gradually more and more of the building was involved. If we think of the new skyscrapers in the U.S.A., which use prefabricated panels, prefabricated windows, prefabricated surface plates and ready-made curtain walls, then we can rest assured that the architect is beginning to have a different role. This is certainly not valid everywhere, for if the same architect designs a cabin on the top of an isolated mountain he may still be working in the same way as the architect, or rather the mason, of earlier times. However, between the architect who has to work almost entirely with prefabricated materials and the one who has to work only with natural materials, there is a whole range of solutions which prove that the modern architect is being forced to move from an architecture which was a product of handicraft to one which has become an industrial product. At the same time the number of people participating directly or indirectly in the creation of a building becomes larger and larger and moves towards the infinite (Fig. 3).

BETWEEN LOCAL AND INTERNATIONAL

The gradual trend from handicraft production to industrial pro-

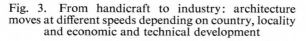

Fig. 3. From handicraft to industry: architecture
moves at different speeds depending on country, locality
and economic and technical development

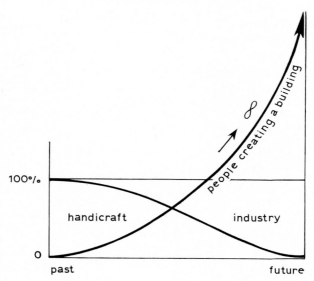

duction also implies a shift of architectural solutions from the local
towards the international level. If certain materials are produced
only in some countries, then the people designing those materials
will exercise an influence in the country where the building incor-
porating them is to stand. Architecture thus moves between the local
and the international, and architects are permanently caught between
these two competing groups of forces (Fig. 4).

International co-operation on matters of development is a very
recent phenomenon, and experience in this field is limited. We are
all still at the experimental stage of this new attempt to foster a
better understanding among people and create a better world. Taken
together with the other elements of our age, the acceptance of all the
principles we have here mentioned inevitably leads towards a similarity of solutions in different parts of the world. These similarities
have been caused by three waves of influences.

The first wave was raised by the creation of mechanical means of
production or transportation, which are used everywhere in similar

Fig. 4.   Architecture moves from local to international,
and the architect is caught between these two forces

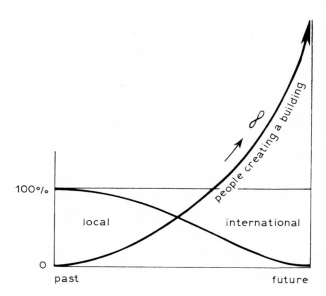

manner, and the similarities began to be apparent in particular kinds
of buildings, such as certain types of industrial plants which have to
house a standard type of function. A mill, to take one example, could
be designed in London and built in exactly the same way in many
parts of the world. This was true especially if the climates of these
areas were all similar, although the same could also apply if the
climates differed, provided that allowance were made for air-heating,
air-cooling or even air-conditioning. Regardless of region or town
there are functions—particularly in the field of communications—
which are based on standards of a more or less universal nature.
For instance, we have built the same types of railway stations to
house the same types of locomotives, the same types of garage and
the same types of buildings for harbours and airports which are to
serve the same types of ships and aeroplanes throughout the world;
furthermore, the petrol companies began selling from a standard type
of petrol station which has now become ubiquitous; and so the
process continues.

The second wave of similar solutions began when materials produced in one country, such as prefabricated doors, windows and panels, began to be sold and used in another. The advent of prefabricated furniture has even led to a similarity in types of interior furnishing and decoration. Later, with the growth of communications, came the spread of fashions; conceived in one country but able to influence other parts of the world through magazines, books, films, television and so on.

Finally, there were the universities of the highly developed part of the Western world producing architects, who thereupon spread all over the world. In their turn, these represented a third force leading to a similarity of solutions.

At the beginning of human history there was no tradition of any importance. Similar solutions occurred in different localities because people were perhaps the same and equally equipped for architectural creation and because they were using similar materials in similar surroundings. Local, regional and then international radiation began. Is this radiation going to become so strong as to destroy the local growths?

There was, of course, a justifiable reaction to this trend towards similarity, for buildings could not be the same irrespective of climate, locality or local traditions. The people who had learned the new approach in the Western universities were simply mimicking the solutions worked out at their schools and were not adapting their approach to the new environment. Many mistakes were thus made; and we have seen, and may still see, numerous buildings throughout the world which fail to serve the people at all because they have been transplanted from a different country and a different environment.

Two movements thereupon came into conflict. The first, arising out of mechanization and standardization, led to a similarity of solutions. The other opposed it, on the ground that these solutions were being imposed without regard to climatic and local considerations.

As conditions stand at present it is quite probable that these movements, the one leading to a similarity of solutions and the other leading to local solutions, are both valid for most of the countries of the world. The wisdom of the choice between them will depend on the relative importance to be given to these two tendencies at any specific moment, for any specific type of building. Let us take

C

Islamabad, the new capital of Pakistan, as an example. During the early sixties the economy of Pakistan will require the use of local materials as far as physically possible, and in these conditions several of the universal forces will exert no influence whatsoever, since the local materials will be those which will influence the buildings. If we speak of Islamabad in the seventies, however, then the situation will be different, and it will be far more different one or two generations later.

FACING QUANTITATIVE PROBLEMS

All our thinking up to now has been directed to the problem of quality and it must be confessed that, when talking about architecture, architect and layman alike confine themselves almost exclusively to qualitative problems. We talk of what we like, what is best, what is rational, and seldom think of the big quantitative problems we have to face. Even more seldom do we try to combine the qualitative with the quantitative problems.

Looking around, however, we do not see merely the distance between academic and modern. We discover that the large masses of people are not interested even in talking about the differences between old and new, nor do they care whether architecture is moving from handicraft to industrial production, or whether we are dealing with local or international factors. In fact, these are problems which the experts must discuss and which only a limited number of persons can in fact understand. The large masses of people are really interested in their way of life, but when talking about architecture they confine themselves to a cursory and superficial examination of our architectural production, our habitat and our cities. They look mainly to the appearance of architecture. However, if we proceed to look not at the façades of our buildings but inside, into the heart of our architecture, we shall discover that the homeless or poorly housed millions who constitute the majority of the people on the earth, live under very bad conditions indeed (Fig. 5).

But we must take yet another step and see that it is not merely that the majority of mankind is ill-housed, but that many of our needs are not served at all or are badly served in the wrong kind of buildings or in buildings which are too small and inadequate for our needs.

How do we react to the fact that our building efforts are smaller than the corresponding needs, that they are in fact not comparable at all to the real needs of humanity? Let us be frank. In our talks about architecture we usually forget the greatest number of our potential clients, that is, we usually forget the quantitative questions related to architecture, considering them to have no influence on the situation. But what percentage of the people, in fact, have the privilege of a proper house or a proper school building? We do not think of that, nor do we relate it to the problems of quality.

If we decide to do so, we must recognize that we have quantitative as well as qualitative problems to tackle, and that the quantitative problems should not be left to one side while we devote our attention mainly to the qualitative ones. If this bias continues, then we are doomed to remain in the epoch of transition. We will be unable to find any way out and, what is worse, our efforts to serve our real clients, that is, the population of the whole earth, will be a complete

Fig. 5.   The greatest part of humanity lives in conditions similar to these. This is the main architectural problem

failure. How can we believe that we create an architecture when the solutions given are only good or possible for a certain very small class of people which may exist in all countries or only in some of them, but which nevertheless constitutes a minority in relation to the great masses of people we have to serve?

It is high time for us to recognize that in this epoch of transition our goal cannot be to create architecture in the abstract, but to dedicate our architectural creation to the service of the people.

FROM MEGALOMANIA TO REALISM

If we study the real dimensions of our problem we shall discover that, far from being exaggerated, the above remarks can more properly be termed understatements. Architects are really not influencing architecture, but only a very small part of the total activity. What is worse, humanity itself is not concerned with the problem of architectural creation as a whole, but only with that very small part that relates to its particular needs.

How are we facing problems of such dimensions? Through our schools of architecture. But the spirit prevailing there does not help architects to face our problems. As an example I may mention that most of the schools teach architectural styles, and lay great emphasis on the final achievement of a particular modern style. But what is of interest is not what styles have been created, but rather how styles are created, what the long and difficult road was that humanity had to follow in order to create a particular style. The important thing is the process by which a style is born, its actual birth and not the style in itself. Styles, like the civilizations which create them, rise and fall during the ages: what is important is the study of the dynamics of style-making or style-creation, not of style as a form or an end in itself.

Another example of our failure to face these problems in the proper way is the fact that most of the architectural schools teach very little about low-cost housing, about the great numbers of buildings which are necessary everywhere, and concentrate mainly on the few buildings which are exceptional, either in size or in conception.

It is interesting to note that when we speak about architecture today, whether we open our magazines or look at what is exhibited, we will find that our attention is concentrated on buildings which are not easily repeated, on a theatre, a big university or a big hospital. We overlook the great majority of the buildings which are repeated thousands, hundreds of thousands, even millions, of times and concentrate on exceptional achievements. This is, of course, important if these achievements are indeed exceptional. But to concentrate on them just because they are few and not easily repeated, and overlook the great majority of the efforts of humanity just because they are modest, is completely wrong. It is natural to concentrate on exceptional achievements when these are the embodiment of ideas accumulated during a certain period, the expression of a certain era, or even when they are the idealization of the architecture around us.

During the past few generations—and this is valid of our time also—architects have in general been suffering from megalomania. Each thinks that his job is to create another Taj Mahal or a Parthenon, an approach that is both wrong and wasteful. Can we think of general practitioners as trying only to imitate Pasteur or Koch? What we should understand is that the main task of an architect, like that of a doctor, is to serve his patient on the basis of knowledge already acquired, and that it is only for the very few to investigate and do research in order to achieve progress in theory and implementation.

Thus, when the moment comes for the creation of the proper type of housing for the millions, architects, used as they are to creating only large or monumental buildings, find it very difficult either to undertake the work or to be practical in their creation.

Architects are in fact outside the great movement for the creation of large quantities of houses and other buildings. That job is left to the common man or the common mason, the industrialist or the contractor, with the result that nothing is offered but conformist solutions and a docile imitation of local fashion. Architecture is thus created not by the architects but in spite of them.

It is now high time to admit that we architects have made grave mistakes; instead of being the *avant-garde*, the crusaders in the construction of houses for the masses, we have timidly remained in the background and left others to do our job.

THE REAL QUESTION: HOW WE WANT TO LIVE

Acknowledging all this, we must turn our attention for a moment to something even more substantial than architectural design, and that is the question of *how we live*. We must find an approach to the problem not of how our architecture is to look, but of how it is to serve us. We must indeed admit that we do not live as we would wish to live, so that the even more difficult question arises as to *how we want to live* and what our ideals really are. In asking ourselves this question we have to be careful to define all three of its elements: *we, want, live*.

The first, which is also the most important, presents the notion of democracy and socialization. We can no longer limit our interest to the privileged classes, whether on regional, professional, economic, social or cultural criteria. By 'we' we mean the common man everywhere, who now enters the picture not only to be served by architecture but also to decide about it. This leads in turn to new dimensions for the problem and new techniques for finding solutions.

The second notion, 'want', introduces a very difficult element, as it is, by its nature, a notion very hard to define. Does the want represent the *feeling* of the needs (material and intellectual) of the average citizen, bearing as he does the paralysing weight of his present habitat? Or does it represent the knowledge of the expert, or even the dream of the visionary? How are we to define it?

Finally, the third notion of 'live' also requires proper interpretation. By 'live' do we mean the time we spend inside architecture (buildings), around it (public squares, roads, etc.) or even outside it? After answering these basic queries we can then proceed to more detailed questions: Do we want to live in big cities or small cities, big communities or small communities? What kind of communities do we in fact want? Do we prefer to live in multi-storey buildings or in single-family detached houses or rows of houses? And then, how do we want to move about? Do we want to walk, or move on elevators, escalators or moving paths? Do we perhaps even want to be transported on moving bands within our buildings, as has been proposed lately?

Here it is relevant, surely, to ask ourselves why we have paid greater attention lately to travelling than to living in our homes. How can we justify the fact that many people have a better car than a house; that so many people who would be ashamed to drive an old car in fact live in a dilapidated house? Is this perhaps proof of a trend towards nomadism or simply the inability of our society to face its housing problem? I myself believe it is this second cause which is slowly but surely turning many people into nomads, since there is no proper permanent habitat for them. It is equally timely to ask ourselves why we have been unable to face so many other important problems related to our architecture, such as the structure of our urban communities.

Now, in sum, is the moment to ask ourselves if we can define our ideals for a better way of living. Only if we really know how we want to live, and what our ideals are, can we find answers to our many problems, because only then shall we know what our targets ought to be.

When we have defined our ideals and our needs we can turn our minds to the degree to which we serve those needs. Then we shall recognize that we simply do not serve them satisfactorily, but serve them only to a limited extent, over limited areas and for a limited number of people.

In describing our epoch as one of transition, we asserted that not only architecture but everything in it is characterized by a high rate of change, that everything is in transition and that architecture is merely following the broader trend. We looked into the problem in the way in which architects usually look at it, to find ourselves in a transition from academic to modern, to discover that we have been caught between old and new and to realize that we are not sure of what we mean by new and have to define it. Thus, we moved on to problems related to the substance of architecture, asserting that we are moving from handicraft towards industry in architectural production, that we are caught between local and international forces; above all, that we are facing quantitative problems and that we architects, hindered by megalomania, lack a realistic view of our problems. We then came to the real question of how we want to live, which we need to clarify before we define how we should in fact live.

A generation ago our great problem was how to break with the past, how to break the bonds of centuries and be free to create. Now our problem arises from the fact that we are entangled in a transitional period of humanity and so in a transitional period of architecture. Our problem is that because of this transition we are in a state of confusion from which we must somehow escape before we can go forward again.

Since the role of the architect is changing because of the change of architecture from handicraft to industry, we must make sure that the architect is able to play his new role. He is to be the production architect, who will enter industry and influence it in the right direction, as well as the man who will be able to create a broader synthesis.

As he is now being slowly deprived of many of the worries of everyday design, he need no longer think in detail of every window, every door or every roof. With his help industry will provide answers to these problems, while he will be free to find a new role, i.e. to create better architecture by dedicating more of his time to the overall synthesis from the point of view of rationalism and aesthetics.

We may now be forced to the conclusion that we shall have to deal with two types of architects in the future. The one will turn towards industry and contribute to the production of the elements of the architecture to come. The other, who can influence the industry by describing his requirements exactly while leaving it to others to design and produce them, can expand more into the field of broader creations for the formation of our habitat. We may also be forced to seek other solutions which may even lead to a revolution in our ideas about architecture and architects. We must feel free to do this should it prove necessary, because we are here to serve human needs and not to impose any kind of acquired ideas and disciplines.

3   the causes of the crisis

THE REAL ISSUES

IT IS now obvious that our architectural confusion is due to the stage of transition we are passing through, and that this also constitutes the main problem we have to face. It seems necessary, therefore, to try to find the real causes of this problem. Only then can we define the forces which are at work and the trends which are emerging, and so think clearly about the architecture of the future.

But first we should not be confused by secondary or tertiary causes. If we say, for example, that architecture has not been adjusted in time and that it has been or is still being taught academically, that is a cause of tertiary importance. There are good reasons why architecture has not been adjusted and is not being taught in the proper way, and it is those reasons which are in fact the root cause of the general crisis within which architecture found itself and became confused.

The important issues, the primary causes of transition, are really also basic problems in themselves. The problem of the fast growth of population, for instance, is a cause of many other problems; such as lack of food, lack of shelter, etc. It is in this respect that we may say that the main problems and the causes of the crisis are basically one and the same.

Before embarking on an analysis of our problems and their causes, let us sum up the position. We must reassert that these are of a quantitative and qualitative nature, remembering that in speaking of the real substance of architecture the basic problems are those of

41

people badly housed or not housed at all, and of people very badly served by their existing buildings and their total habitat, whether because of deficiencies in nature, size, shape or appearance. We shall try to analyse our problems on the basis of the *law of cause and effect*, but if we are to understand the new forces which are responsible for the situations that we are finding it so difficult to face, we must first grasp that the causes of our problems in architecture are basically similar to those of many of the problems of our epoch.

Let us try to look at these problems in a quantitative manner; as a result we shall also be led to a fuller understanding of their qualitative aspects.

THE GROWTH OF POPULATION

Our first problem and cause is what is sometimes called the population explosion. The world has never before witnessed such an expansion of its already teeming millions, with the result that while the population grows faster with the development of modern medicine and public health programmes, its increase is not paced by any comparable increase in architectural activity, so that very many people are left without houses and buildings. The very subject of our architecture has itself expanded and has consequently created worse conditions than ever before.

Whenever and wherever there is a growth in population the production of goods lags behind for some time until the whole production machine has geared itself to the increasing need. In architecture, a field of human activity where great and varied production efforts are still required, from building materials to finished architectural products, this lag is perhaps bigger than elsewhere. It was possible in the past for the number of architectural workers to increase at the same rate as the expansion of the population itself, but now a gap exists, and it is this gap that is responsible for an enormous number of our quantitative and qualitative problems (Fig. 6). What happens is that in trying to face a quantitative problem as soon as it arises we do in fact make an increased effort, but, since this is an effort for which we are substantially unprepared, the result is only that the quality of our work as a whole falls off.

The population of the earth is at present increasing at a rate of

Fig. 6. The gap between population and architectural production has been increasing recently and is going to increase
even more in the future

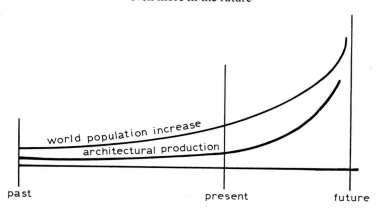

past   present   future

2 per cent per annum. Were this growth our only quantitative
problem, we should still need to increase our output by a minimum
of 2 per cent every year.

ECONOMIC DEVELOPMENT

The second problem and cause of our transitional period is economic
development, which is taking place at an unprecedented rate, whether
considered as the average rate for the whole of humanity, or as a
special rate for particular countries. This rate cannot itself be
estimated with any precision, but it is certainly greater than the rate
of growth of the population. It may be of the order of 3 to 4 per cent
generally, although in some countries it seems that it can even exceed
10 per cent over certain periods.

This acceleration of economic development creates a variety of
new problems which are of the greatest importance for architecture,
for while everyone requires better and better buildings, the demand
for buildings grows at a higher rate than that of the increase of wealth
or the general rate of growth of the economy.

This quantitative economic improvement carries with it a qualitative as well as a quantitative demand. Once the people reach a
higher income level, they ask not only for larger houses or schools,

but also for better and better-equipped ones. What is more, if the people are already properly educated they will demand that their new houses or schools look better aesthetically, too.

SOCIALIZATION

The third basic problem, which is at the same time a fundamental cause of our problems, is the rapid socialization of every aspect of our lives. In the past, even until only one or two generations ago, the architect had to work for priests and kings and nobles, for the House of God or for the mansion of his temporal lord. At times he had to work for civic centres, in cities where the municipality itself assumed responsibility for the central parts of the city, or for individual wealthy citizens who wanted private mansions or villas built to their own specifications.

Now, however, our whole attitude is changing, and the attention of governments, societies and local bodies alike is turning to the service of all citizens. Housing is now to be provided for everybody, and everybody is to be given all the facilities offered by modern society. This is taking place everywhere, regardless of political systems, although at rates varying with the economic development programmes and social policies of the countries concerned, and it amounts to a major change in concepts. Simply put, we no longer build monuments.

If we now remember that because of the lack of proper policies, especially during the Industrial Revolution, large masses of people swarmed into the cities and have remained there without proper facilities in housing, buildings, etc., we can understand what an impact socialization is having on our demand for greater architectural production and for better architecture.

Even if we assume that the population is increasing at a rate of 2 per cent and the per capita income at the rate of 4 per cent per annum, then allowing only 1 per cent for the replacement of buildings, the total annual demand for architecture will be 7 per cent. If architecture is to serve the people, even this increase in its output of 7 per cent per annum leaves us with the sad fact that large masses of people who are now very badly served will remain so for ever.

The conclusion is that the rate at which architectural production should take place should be much larger than the corresponding increase in population and development of the economy.

In many countries experience has taught us that, because erroneous policies were followed, the level of architectural production over the past decade was smaller than the increase in the rate of population growth. In fact, lack of proper social policies and the absence of liberty in the past did not permit the people to voice the total demand for architecture which should have followed the increase of population and the development of the economy.

At present, as the need for architecture becomes all the more apparent, its rate of increase must be higher than that of population growth and the development of the economy. It seems that this ratio will have to remain unchanged for many decades to come, simply to bridge the gaps and discrepancies created in the past. The single factor of rapid socialization alone demands far greater architectural production than at any time before.

To recapitulate. In the past need followed the increase in population, but being suppressed it was expressed as a demand equal only to the supply. In the recent past, however, there was an increase in demand as well as in need; a gap was thus created between the two, a gap which will become larger as the curve of demand comes closer to and at length coincides with the curve of need. This fact is already forcing supply to increase, but it will take many decades or even centuries for demand and supply to reach a point of equilibrium (Fig. 7).

All this means that the gap between need and demand will be closed at some time in the future, while the gap between demand and supply will at first increase. Supply will thus have to increase, eventually at a rate much higher than the increase in population plus the increase in per capita income. This will itself create problems of even greater magnitude in terms of production, not only of the proper numbers of buildings but also of the proper quality of them.

ENTER THE CAR

We have seen how the great problems created by the growth of population are being aggravated by the economic development and rapid socialization of our age. Now a fourth force comes into play.

Fig. 7. Architectural needs are increasing while the demand for architecture is still suppressed and is lagging behind. In the future, however, demand will tend towards actual needs. Thus, the supply will have to be increased; but before we reach this stage the gap between supply and demand will widen

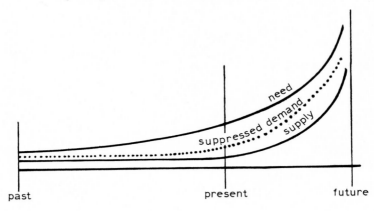

A major cause of our problems is the machine, which has entered our lives once and for all, and with a double effect. Its first effect is due to the changing pattern of transport and is an effect of scale. The style of architecture, which was formerly defined by man alone, is now defined by taking man together with his machines. It is the car that stands central to our concept of the man-machine scale, for the car is the most significant mechanical element to have entered our lives, changing our pattern of transport and thus influencing our architecture.

Formerly there was man, moving at a speed of some three miles an hour; now there is the car, moving at speeds of up to and even over 100 miles an hour, so that man and his motor-car are at odds. He is soft where it is hard, slow where it is fast and small where it is large (Fig. 8).

The motor-car has broken rudely into our lives and elbowed us out of the road, out of our courtyards and squares, even preventing us from looking at our buildings or approaching them in the proper way any longer. By bringing man and motor-car into conflict we have dissatisfied both, for we have broken up the scale of life together with the scale of architecture. Especially have we made man un-happy, for he has become a mere displaced person within his own city. But we have made our cars—or rather their drivers—unhappy too, for, although designed for much greater speed, our cars are compelled to cross the city of man at speeds such as six miles an hour in cities like Glasgow or ten miles an hour in cities like London.

The effects of this situation on architecture are numerous. Primarily, we have lost public space. In Los Angeles two-thirds of the central part of the city is covered by cars, whether parked or in motion (Fig. 9). Because of this change in the distribution of open space in relation to buildings, man has lost his normal relationship to architecture. Our buildings are no longer directly related to man, for in many parts of our greatest cities they appear to be floating in a

Fig. 8.   The car enters the picture and changes the scale of dimensions which was previously controlled only by man

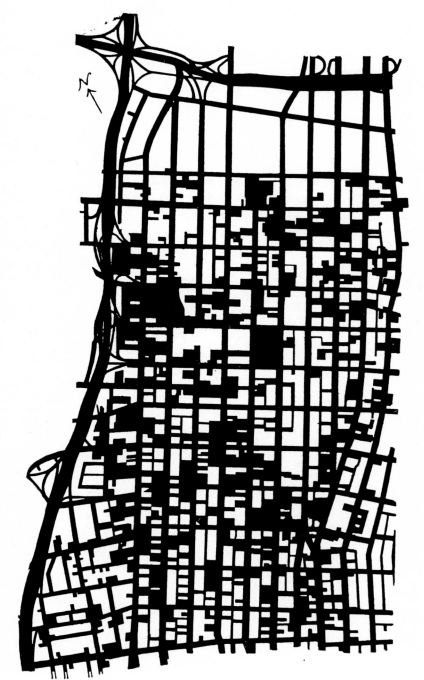

Fig. 9. Two-thirds of the central part of Los Angeles is taken over by cars
either moving or parked

Fig. 10. Positive and negative syntheses

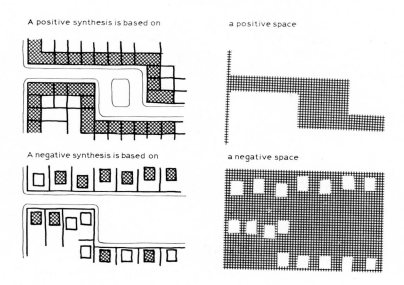

A positive synthesis is based on   a positive space

A negative synthesis is based on   a negative space

lake of cars. Our monuments and statues, too, can no longer be seen in their proper perspective because of the break in relationship between human beings and their normal surroundings.

The second effect of this irruption of the motor-car is that in many countries people are tending to live at greater distances from the city. In gaining the facility of travelling home by car they have broken the architectural unity which previously existed by building detached houses with great distances between them, in gardens where they are isolated from one another in the rural landscape. Thus spaces are formed which in the end have a negative character.

The space within our urban landscape formerly had a positive form; whether square or circular, it had its own characteristic shape. Now, however, space has in many places taken on a negative and not a positive character. That is a grave mistake on our part (Fig. 10).

What is more, the car has already been followed by another machine which is influencing our pattern of life. This is the aeroplane, and it is soon to be followed by the rocket. So the man-scale for defining our relationship to architecture has now become a scale of man, car, aeroplane and rocket.

D

For one master we have substituted four, and these are breaking up the space in which we live and create our architecture. In so doing, they are creating even greater problems for us (Fig. 11).

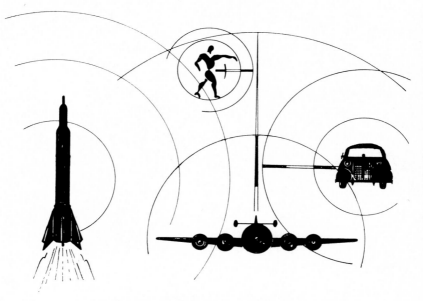

Fig. 11.   The human scale of our cities has now been replaced by many scales, of which the human is the weakest

INDUSTRIALIZATION AND TECHNOLOGICAL PROGRESS

The fifth cause of our problems is industrialization and technological progress, both of which have contributed to the growth of architecture in the third dimension of height and depth. Because of them we now have skyscrapers as an element in our architectural environment and, consequently, new problems in both technology and architecture.

Industrialization and technology have given us buildings moving into the third dimension not only in height but also in depth, for there is considerable exploitation of the sub-surface possibilities offered within every city. This exploitation, which takes place under buildings as well as under public spaces, provides for

means of transportation, community facilities, installations, etc.
   In these circumstances the traditional methods and simpler types
of construction with which we were formerly content are gradually

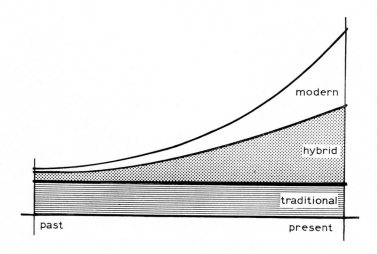

Fig. 12.   Total architectural activity

giving way to a complex architecture in which only modern methods
and materials can exist.
   Between these two types of architecture there occur many hybrids
of traditional and modern methods, raising a host of technical and
aesthetic problems in architectural creation (Fig. 12).
   For the first time in our history the third dimension is playing a
very important role in the creation of the total architectural shape of
our cities. Besides the other new factors in our task we now have to
face the third physical dimension, which starts in effect as a technological one. The complexity of problems which it creates forces
architecture out of the era of handicraft, even supposing it could
have managed to remain there with only one-, two- or three-storey
buildings to build.

URBANIZATION

The sixth basic cause of our problems is urbanization. Urbanization is the result of the previous forces of population growth, economic development and socialization, as well as of industrialization and modern means of transport. In itself, however, it constitutes the major cause of all our problems, for it has completely altered the scale and environment of our architectural creation.

The population is not evenly spread through the countryside today, but is much denser in the urban areas. A most cursory examination of the population trends already apparent in several countries, and latent or emerging in others, establishes that we must expect a slowing down in the rate of increase for the countryside, which will later on lead to a decrease in population there. In the minor urban centres, on the other hand, the rate of increase is noticeably higher than the average for the country as a whole, while in the larger urban areas there is an even larger rate of increase (Fig. 13).

The situation which I have already described is typical of the world as a whole or of any country at an intermediate phase of development. In many countries, however, there have lately been cases where the population as a whole is increasing sharply. In such cases the trends of urbanization are even stronger. The population of the countryside is decreasing while the urban areas are gaining population at a much greater speed.

All this shows that where we have greater needs for architecture we shall encounter greater problems.

Most of our buildings are now created within urban areas, and architecture is of course influenced by its new environment. We have already seen that architecture has reached out both in height and depth, but this is not the only, or even the major, phenomenon of architecture in the urban areas. There is its conflict with modern means of transportation, but there is also the fact that in the growing urban areas those buildings of the past which gave their cities a monumental character, buildings such as churches, city halls, palaces or monuments, are now passing to secondary importance within the city. This is simply because they were conceived as buildings only a few storeys high. The church is no longer the tallest building in

Fig. 13.   World population: tending towards stability by about the end of the twenty-first century; rural population is steadily decreasing until it will finally disappear

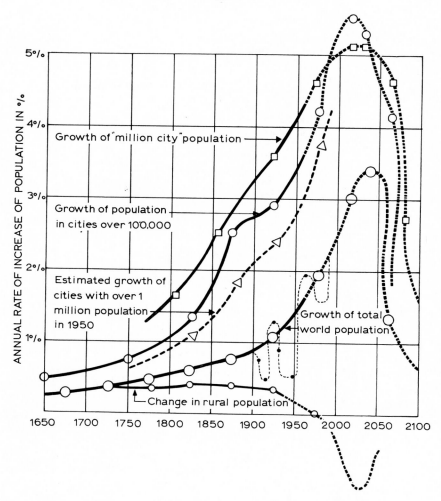

the city, and the same applies to all our monumental buildings. Thus the direct influence exerted by these buildings on the people is declining, while at the same time their very function as symbols is itself diminishing in importance because they have lost their significance in the scale of the city.

The large buildings of the past which were of a monumental nature constituted at the same time the major elements of the city, controlling its rhythm and imposing their character on it. Now they have become relatively small, and thus their influence is correspondingly so lessened that we can already feel the gap. We need only look at a church within a growing city, hidden between much taller buildings, to realize that what was originally a convex city skyline whose salient features were the city's monumental buildings, has been metamorphosed into a concave one in which those same buildings have been dwarfed into insignificance (Fig. 14).

There is thus a big change in our architectural background. These monumental buildings were formerly the real city, for, as Sir Christopher Wren said, 'Architecture has its political use, public buildings being the ornament of the country; it establishes a nation, draws people and commerce and makes the people love their native country, which passion is the original of all great actions in a commonwealth.' Today these public buildings are small, but even that is not the worst of it. These buildings were always conceived as monumental, and as such were planned on introvert, closed schemes, schemes which cannot stand expansion. The functions they serve, however, must and do undergo a continuous expansion. Let us think for only a moment of our universities, colleges, hospitals and other buildings around us which we all know, and consider what their needs will be twenty or even only ten years from now. Their needs will certainly be greater, but since many of these buildings have been conceived in monumental styles, with introvert schemes, they cannot stand expansion and so will be unable to serve their purpose any longer.

It is the conception of monumentality in buildings that has led to introvert forms, and it is these forms which in their turn have arrested the possibility of normal growth and normal expansion in the function of many of our buildings, thus creating bad architecture. The resultant rigid and unexpandable forms are left on our hands, like fossils.

COEXISTENCE OF MANY FORCES

The seventh and final cause of our problems is the very coexistence of all the above-mentioned forces of population growth, economic

Fig. 14.   Monumental buildings which were the apex of architecture are now buried between commercial buildings

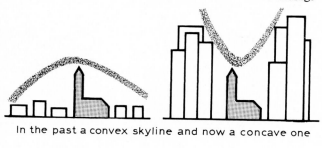

In the past a convex skyline and now a concave one

Monumentality led to introverted forms and these have left us with fossils

development, socialization, mechanization of transport, industrialization, technological progress and urbanization in the same age and the same areas.

Let us try to understand just how great the changes are which result from this coexistence of all the factors we have analysed. We have a growth of population, to which must be added the factor of greater income. For an average population growth of 2 per cent per annum we assume an annual growth in per capita income of 4 per cent, which results in a 6 per cent yearly increase in demand for architectural creation. If we add 1 per cent for replacement of existing buildings the total is 7 per cent. Socialization, the expansion of the subject, may increase this 6 per cent by an additional 2, 3 or even 4 per cent, to cover the needs which have been accumulated in the past, even over one generation. All this adds up to a total of 11 per cent per annum, even if socialization takes a long time to achieve its basic goals.

Now this 11 per cent for a country in fact means much more in the urban areas, because the growth of population, income and socialization are moving at a greater speed in the urban than in the rural areas, a factor which may result in an increase of as much as 15 or 17 per cent in the need for architectural creation in the urban

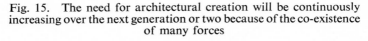

Fig. 15. The need for architectural creation will be continuously increasing over the next generation or two because of the co-existence of many forces

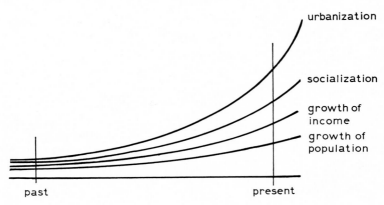

areas over the next generation or two (Fig. 15). If we compare these figures with the growing problems, the problems arising out of new techniques and other new factors entering our lives, we shall begin to appreciate the true size of the difficulties before us.

Now it is natural to ask whether these ever-growing problems which we first presented as quantitative do not have their influence on the qualitative problems too.

We have only to remember that if we spread socially we shall acquire different needs, and shall have to go back to simpler forms of expansion. After all, there is a world of difference between the concept of working for the few in creating a limited number of monuments, and that of working for the many, who require not monumental buildings but services. We have only to consider, for instance, how the tentacular spread of our suburbs over the country-side brings us into contact with nature, but how we break up our architectural creation by creating what are in effect negative spaces and so heap fresh difficulties upon our own heads.

We have only to consider how the impact of the transport machine is changing our patterns of life, so that in spilling out as we are into space because of economic growth we are reaching new areas, rural areas and in a broader sense also underdeveloped areas, which have never been served before. It is natural that this process should bring into play new geographic concepts such as that of other types of climate, and that these new concepts should require new thinking and new solutions.

The coexistence and interplay of all these many forces we have referred to often compel man to make a sudden leap from a nomadic or rural pattern of life into a modern industrialized system. A shepherd or farmer may have to become an industrial worker overnight, that is, a free organism in nature has to become a disciplined social being. This is only one example of the colossal strain which is placed on people today, forcing us to seek new solutions in architecture in order to save man from the breakdown with which his new ways of living are threatening him.

Evidence of this strain can be seen in practically all the areas where architecture is now being created in rapidly developing countries, where alien—and not necessarily good—kinds of architecture have been imported. In most of the cases that we could mention the architecture created within the urban areas, or in the suburbs of the cities of developing countries, is an architecture which has simply been transplanted there. Such an architecture does not have, and can never have, firm roots in the country.

But even in countries where an architectural tradition already existed, the problems have been very great. We can understand how important the changing rate of growth is if we look at some of our cities. For instance, the area of Athens, the birthplace of Western civilization, was never inhabited by more than 200,000 people for a period of thousands of years, but suddenly mushroomed, within a mere fifty-year period, to contain almost 2,000,000 people. Similar cases could be cited throughout the world to show how large the cumulative effect of all these forces is. To remember that the building wealth created in Athens during the last fifty years alone is forty times as great as that created during the entire classical period is to be impressed yet again with the significance of the changing rate of growth (Fig. 16).

It is now clear that we are at present dealing with a dynamic situation which creates a host of problems for every aspect of our lives, and with them new demands for architectural creation. These problems range from the most practical and quantitative ones to

Fig. 16. The population of Athens

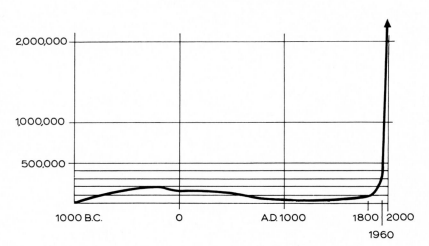

those involving cultural and aesthetic values. In order to understand how great is the variety of these problems, and how we are forced to change our views about architecture, let us examine two particular cases, that of urban housing and that of public buildings, and try to understand some of the fresh problems which they create.

A NEW OUTLOOK FOR URBAN HOUSES

An increase in population, especially in the urban areas, obviously demands a much larger production of houses. Then industrialization implies, even demands, that people should be mobile between area and area, town and town, neighbourhood and neighbourhood, so that the working population can be adjusted to the location of its employment. The forces of socialization, on their part, demand that whatever measures we take must be taken for everybody, so that we must stretch our resources over greater and greater numbers of people. Economic limitations, on the other hand, compel us to apply these same resources first and foremost to what is indispensable, and to make the greatest possible economies, for the broad masses of people would otherwise simply remain without facilities altogether. We are thus led to the conception of national housing programmes, which divide the total architectural activity in a rational way for every country, at each phase of its development (Fig. 17).

We must now turn to the life-cycle of the family. It begins as a small unit of two, then grows to a climax, then falls off and finally

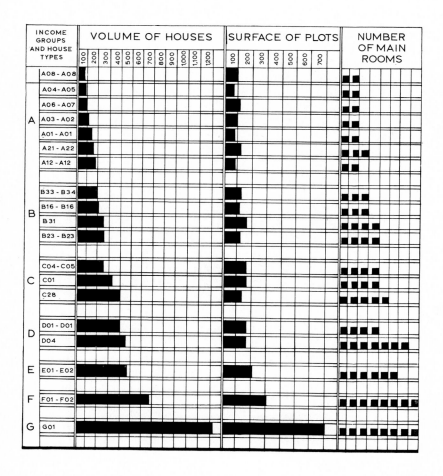

Fig. 17.   The National Housing Programme of Iraq, 1955, gives an example of a rational housing programme for a transitional phase of the development of Iraq. It provides all types of needs and all income groups with a corresponding size of plots and houses (Doxiadis Associates)

becomes smaller and smaller until it becomes extinct. Applying here the criterion of the best possible economy, we conclude that it is unreasonable for us to build a house at its final size right from the beginning. What we need is a house which will grow as the family grows and then contract as it contracts. If we follow the life-cycle of the family we shall find that at the beginning we may need a small unit, let us say of two rooms for a small family of low income. One unit can be added when children come, making four rooms, the addition of a further unit later making a total of six rooms in all.

Then the time comes when two of the three units once more suffice, so that the third can be taken away and given to a second family. When the size of the initial family decreases still further we could dispose of a second unit too, giving this to the second family or even to a third one. Later, the first family disappears from the picture entirely, and the second family grows and may take over the whole house, perhaps at the cost of pushing the other families out. When it begins to contract in its turn, this second family begins to be displaced again by another, which then commences to grow until it gains complete control of the house (Fig. 18).

Such ideas change the whole concept of a house, and we must ask ourselves whether we want to build houses to which we can add or from which we can take away parts at will, or whether we want to tackle the situation in some other way, let us say by co-operative ownership of houses or flats, within which transfers can take place according to the needs of the family, or by public ownership of all houses. This is something which must be viewed within the overall perspective of an architecture still to come.

The fact is that in the past we could afford, in catering for upper-middle-class families, to build private houses which were large from the very beginning and could remain so even if inhabited by a comparatively small family, or even by the last survivor of a family, together with his servants. But then in those days the majority of families had no decent house at all, and that is a situation we cannot afford in the world today.

We can now understand why the architecture of the urban house no longer means the designing of the urban house. It means much more, including the economics of the urban house, which requires

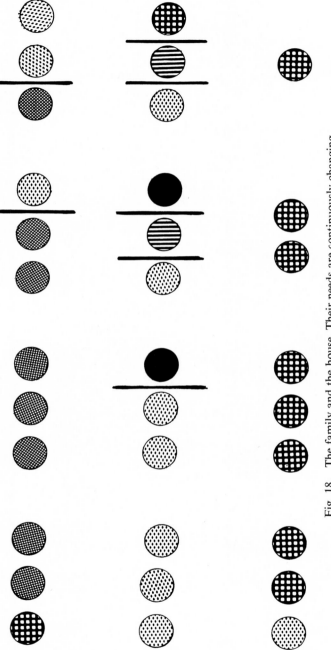

Fig. 18. The family and the house. Their needs are continuously changing. (Every circle represents two rooms)

a new conception for its creation and construction. We have now, for example, to think of the growing house, a house which will start as a small nucleus and will continue to be built over a generation or two. We have to think of the construction of a house on a pre-fabricated basis, that is, of a house which can be bought in pieces at the factory. We have to think of the house which will be built by a co-operative effort, the government or some agency putting up the frame and private people adding their own labour for its completion. Although they cannot afford to pay for a complete house in cash, private individuals can afford to put many man-hours of work into many of the parts of their own future house. This is certainly valid for the rural areas of many countries as it was in most cases in the past, and it begins to be valid again today in urban areas too. If we think in such terms architecture takes on a broader meaning, inside which constructional methods, the economics of such houses and the agent who takes the initiative of carrying through such a plan, will all have an enormous influence.

Architecture is expanding in scope to include new conceptions of architectural building activity. By expanding its scope it is also changing those aspects of its task which are directly related to design, and even to aesthetics.

A NEW OUTLOOK FOR PUBLIC BUILDINGS

Our second case is rather different from that of urban houses. Here we have to face many problems related to the growth of the community, the growth of the demands of the community and the ability of the community to pay for a certain public building.

Let us take the case of an elementary school which has just been created in a community. This school will most probably have to start operating with a student body which is below normal strength. Then the community will grow and the school building will have to expand, adding more rooms for its increasing numbers of children, until it reaches the maximum possible number of rooms, each of which will correspond to one class. At the same time, however, if the income of the community is increasing, the school will have to add extra rooms for special types of lessons, laboratories, libraries, auditoriums, etc., which may not have been included in the original construction.

In the case of a house, if the family outgrows the initial expectation of its size or outgrows its income it simply moves into another house or another neighbourhood. This is not possible, however, for a public building. Its location is defined by community needs. Even more, the investment which has already been made and the value of land are such that it is usually difficult to find space for another school within a certain community. In most cases the school must grow around its initial nucleus.

In this respect the creation of an architecture to serve a school or any other type of public building is much more difficult, and in the same way the architecture of public buildings of all kinds is now a more demanding task. The architect must have the imagination and ability to foresee not only as much as can be foreseen in the circumstances—in this case, what will have to be added to a school later even if this cannot be financed from the beginning—but he must also be able to predict those needs which cannot, by the nature of the case, be foreseen at all clearly. I mean such needs as will result from the changing conception of the needs for educational buildings which is natural in a society that is changing its views about its whole civilization.

We need only consider how our notions of particular community buildings have changed over the past years—our notions, say, of health centres, community centres or markets—to appreciate that what is valid for a school building is going to be valid, and to an even greater extent, for all other types of buildings serving the community.

THE NEW DIMENSION OF TIME

If we now try to pinpoint the main characteristic in a situation which has so radically altered the framework in which our architecture is created, we shall see that what has really changed is our notion of time.

Of course the population would have grown, of course socialization was already on the move and of course the machine had already been introduced into our lives; but the changes which these phenomena caused were all taking place at a very much slower tempo. Our needs were certainly increasing in the past, but much more

Fig. 19.   Architecture in a changing world: the gap between the change of economic and social phenomena and
architectural creation is increasing

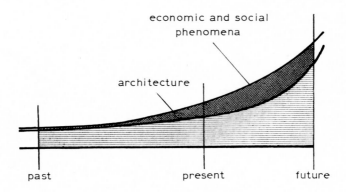

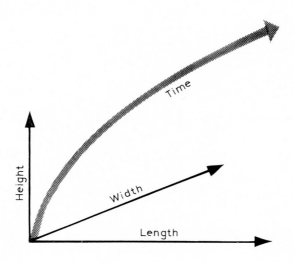

Fig. 20.   The dimension of time now plays the
most important role in architectural creation

slowly. What is really different in our age, then, is the tempo of change, which has already been expressed in population and in social and economic phenomena but not in architecture. That is how the gap has been created (Fig. 19).

Summing up all this in another way, we might say that the basic problem of architecture today is the addition of the dimension of time to the three-dimensional synthesis we have had to handle up to now (Fig. 20). In place of static situations involving slow change we are now caught up in dynamic situations bringing the most rapid changes in their train, and this is what makes the radical difference in the present situation and outlook for architecture.

Architecture in our era has had to conquer this fourth dimension of time. In doing so, it has been forced to change technologically and to make major adjustments. Moving from the period in which it was the two- and, to a very small degree, the three-dimensional domain of the craftsman, architecture now has to adapt itself to the new conditions which the growth of the third dimension and the growing factor of the fourth dimension, the dimension of time, has brought on to the scene.

E

4   architects and architecture

IT IS clear by now that we are in a period of complete architectural confusion in the realm of both ideas and action, and this is definitely due to the fact that we are passing through an epoch of transition. This transition hinders us from clarifying our ideas, primarily because we live with many of the forms of the past, even though the conditions under which these were created have ceased to exist.

Transition is a feature not only of our architecture but of every aspect of life. It is vain to hope that we are going to be done with this soon, and we must therefore adjust ourselves to the idea that we are going through a period of transition and that the causes of the crisis will be with us for many decades or generations to come. The situation may even worsen. Indeed, we can easily predict that in the majority of cases, in most countries, conditions will in fact become steadily worse. We can therefore realistically speak of our increasing problems as a tide, a tide which is rising so rapidly that it threatens humanity, architecture and architects alike.

It will be interesting to see how the average man, the man in the street, faces this tide. He certainly feels the need for the services of architecture, but also feels the growing problems, which he cannot analyse or grasp. He suffers if he has no house, not being able to afford one in his city. He suffers within his community, which is losing its home-like character, just as he suffers within the present-day metropolis because he cannot adjust himself to the new requirements thrust upon him. What is worse, he cannot even express his views on the lack of houses and appropriate buildings, because he cannot speak in specific terms. He cannot even raise his voice to cry out the utter impossibility of the cities he lives in. The rising tide threatens to engulf him.

And what is the position of the architect, the expert, the leader in architecture? He does raise his voice, although we must confess that he raises it very seldom. But even when his voice is raised it has not the power and the strength to awaken the citizens, much less to solve their problems and help them to avoid the tide.

Thus the rising tide will overwhelm humanity, for men will one day discover that they have become the slaves of their surroundings, compelled as they were to adapt themselves to the new conditions of living in a metropolis which is itself dying a slow death under the impact of the machine.

THE ARCHITECT'S RESPONSIBILITY

We have now to clarify how great the architect's responsibility is. We must assume either that he is responsible for leadership in the field of architecture—and its end-product, the way of life of the people—or that he has no responsibility in this field and is merely following the trends which humanity as a whole imposes on him.

We certainly cannot accept the view that the architect has no responsibility in the field of architectural creation. But neither can we expect him to become a dictator. Nobody has this right, even in his own field. Humanity reserves to itself the final decision on such major issues as its way of life, its arts and its architecture. The architect does not have the last word, and in any case he cannot impose his will on the community. On the other hand he is not free to sit idle and simply follow developments as they come.

It is clear that the architect—as the expert in the field of architecture—has one great responsibility: namely, to study contemporary problems and propose solutions for them. By contemporary problems we mean not merely the problems of architectural design in the narrow sense but the broader problems of architecture within a developing society. It is the architect, then, who should study the situation developing around him. interpret it in terms of architecture, present his conclusions in the form of buildings and designs and texts, explain the necessity for a new architectural creation and fight for the right cause.

If he does this properly he will understand that up to a certain point he is bound to follow the general trends of his epoch. The architect has, for example, no right to oppose industrialization and standardization, because these are general forces now in full development serving humanity towards its goals of socialization and the raising of standards of living. The architect has to understand the meaning of industrialization and standardization for the sake of his own creation, and must be prepared to create an architecture which corresponds to the general trends of humanity. His role is to produce the best that can be achieved inside these trends, and not to reverse the general trends themselves. On the other hand, he must not accept them as facts which no longer allow him to create anything better. True, he may not design without standardized elements where industry has already succeeded the artisan: but neither need he accept the industrial product as it is without trying to improve it for his own architectural purposes. This leads to the simple conclusion that the architect will one day have to enter industry and produce his building inside the factory, instead of waiting for the architectural products to be produced by the mechanical engineer or the industrial designer without his contribution.

Similarly, it is not up to the architect to decide whether we are right in moving towards the socialization of our way of life. He has no right to dedicate himself exclusively to the creation of monumental buildings, as he did in the past. It is his responsibility to understand the necessity for socialization in the society of the present and the future, and to adjust his own architecture to serve the broader goals now set by humanity for greater numbers of people and for a better way of life generally.

Or, taking another example, we can say that it is not the architect's role to say, 'Let us get rid of the car!' It is his role and his responsibility to understand that the car, like the machine, is here to stay (unless it is succeeded by some other means of transport), though not as the master of our architecture or our way of life, but as our servant.

Can the architect work towards this goal? If he can, then he is rising to meet his responsibility. If he cannot, he is failing to meet it.

Nor is it the architect's right to stand against urbanization in general or try to conceive ceilings for the growth of settlements.

Urbanization is a trend which is due to many other forces outside the architect's responsibility and beyond his power. Urbanization, the result of so many irreversible forces, is here to stay and we must simply take it for granted. The architect's task is to look at this phenomenon realistically, to recognize it as one of the needs of humanity and to try to serve it as well as he can. Whether he succeeds or not, he should realize that whereas in the past he had to work on a smaller scale, he must now create an architecture for great urban settlements and groups of settlements.

Finally, it is not the architect's role to reverse the natural trends of growing populations and economic development, but to understand them and prepare his total activity in order to serve a growing mass of people whose incomes are increasing and who, as a result, require more and better services from the architect.

Moreover, it is his responsibility to appraise the rising tide around him with an expert's eye and try to regulate it in order to help humanity as well as he can on the road it is taking. The future is being moulded by forces beyond the expert, perhaps beyond man himself. The architect's role is in fact to foresee the broad trends of the evolution which humanity is following and try to create the best possible architecture for the present generation and the generations to come. His role is to understand the future, to foresee it as far as possible and to create the best human habitat for the types of people and for the types of situation which are developing. In this respect the architect's role is different from that of the ekistician, the planner of human settlements; while the architect is building for a maximum of say three generations, the ekistician, who deals with human settlements as a whole, is planning for the future. Although some of the buildings of the architect will survive the era during which they were built, they still constitute short-lived manifestations of the present. On the contrary, the ekistician should have his gaze on the future while at the same time not forgetting that his work should also correspond to the actual needs and possibilities of the present.

THE ARCHITECT'S INFLUENCE

If it now seems clear that the architect has a great responsibility towards humanity we must be equally clear in defining what his influence is. Has he really such an influence as will allow him to play a leading role in the evolution of architecture? Let us examine his sphere of influence, both quantitatively and qualitatively.

The architect is dealing with a total area which is not less than the whole of the earth. This being so, it is inevitable that his qualitative influence should itself be greatly affected by his quantitative influence. We must begin, therefore, by looking into the quantitative influence that the architect exercises on the architecture of our times.

Let us take the total creation in the field of architecture as a single cone, at the base of which are the simplest buildings and at the summit of which are the largest and most monumental ones (Fig. 21). We can now make some statements based on a general knowledge of the situation throughout the world.

The architect operates in

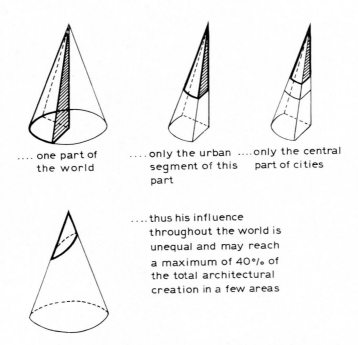

.... one part of the world

.... only the urban segment of this part

....only the central part of cities

....thus his influence throughout the world is unequal and may reach a maximum of 40% of the total architectural creation in a few areas

Fig. 21.   The influence of the architect on total architectural creation

Only one segment of the whole of this cone of architectural creation is at present in the hands of the architect, and that is the urban segment. Of this urban segment, again only the centre of the city is actually in the hands of the architect, and even there it is only the higher expressions which are under his direct and personal control.

If we now turn our attention to the total volume of the architect's influence throughout the world we shall see that we are in effect referring to only a very small part of our cone. The fact that such a very small part of the total building activity throughout the world is under the direct influence of the architect may seem strange to us, but it is a picture which is entirely justified. In fact, the architect's influence over large areas of the globe is precisely nil. It is very small, too, in many developing countries, and reaches a maximum of only 40 per cent even in some areas like England.

There is a second zone of projects which are influenced by the architect and a third one including those projects where architecture is misinterpreted. These are additional categories, but this by no means implies a better architectural creation, quite the contrary.

The total activity of the architect throughout the world is quantitatively very small indeed. What is more, if we bear in mind that architecture is more often than not created on the basis of a town plan, having no architectural conception whatever, we must necessarily conclude that its total effect on the creation of new space is even smaller than our most optimistic estimates.

Let us now try to estimate how big the quantitative influence of the architect really is. Exact data are not available but it is possible to assume that the average density of architects is five per 100,000 of population. This is based on data known for nineteen countries (Fig. 22) where an attempt has been made to relate architects to population and income. If we assume that for each income group these nineteen countries represent the averages of all countries of the same income group, then we may conclude that the total number of architects today is about 150,000.

Assuming, moreover, that the services provided by architects in the United Kingdom—where, as we know, they design about 40 per cent of all buildings—must be matched by architects all over the world, then there is a need for over 1,100,000 architects. This means

RELATIONSHIP BETWEEN PER CAPITA INCOME IN $ AND ARCHITECTS PER 100,000 POPULATION IN SELECTED COUNTRIES

(Year 1959 for Per Capita Income – Year 1958, 1959, 1960 for Architects)

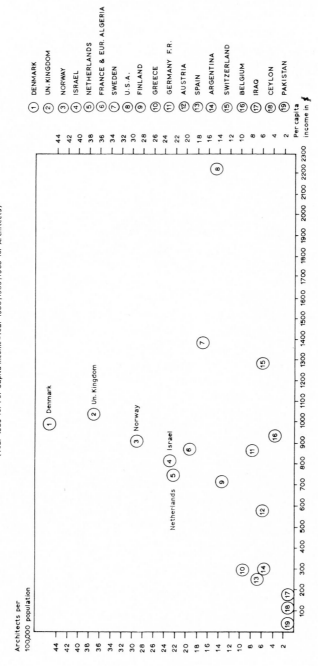

Fig. 22. Architects in relation to national incomes

that there is a deficit of 950,000 (Fig. 23). And if we finally assume that all buildings have to be designed by architects, then the total number required is about 2,800,000, which in turn means a deficit of 2,650,000.

The previous assumptions, which are indeed very liberal, imply that existing architects do not design more than 5 per cent of all buildings created all over the world. It is much more probable that they really control much less, perhaps no more than 2 per cent, because in many countries their numbers do not correspond to the averages assumed and because they tend to take other jobs in government, planning, etc., with consequent reduction in their designing activities (Fig. 24). Even this assumption of 2 per cent is misleading if we think of real architectural creation, which does not mean designing buildings but creating urban architectural space by the combination of all buildings in a certain area. This is certainly not accomplished for more than a millionth of our total architectural creation.

Thus, if we look at architecture in space, we shall see that its direct influence applies only to some very small islands. It is true that it influences some larger areas indirectly; but it is questionable whether its indirect influence in those areas is in fact of a beneficial and not rather of a harmful nature (Fig. 25).

Let us now look at our problem from another standpoint. We have said that it is questionable whether the architect has a direct influence over the architectural space of one millionth of what is created and that he may be designing a maximum of 2 per cent of all the buildings created in the world every year.

What happens to the remaining buildings? The truth of the matter is that most buildings have been created, and are still being created, by people who have had no architectural training of any kind; that is, by the inhabitants themselves or their masons or sometimes their master masons.

In the past these people had everything in their hands, with the exception of those few special or monumental buildings which belonged to the domain of the great master masons. Gradually, however, the intrusion of another species of architect, the architect coming from the schools, has created three distinct categories within the conception of architecture.

The first broad category is still the largest, and, although losing on

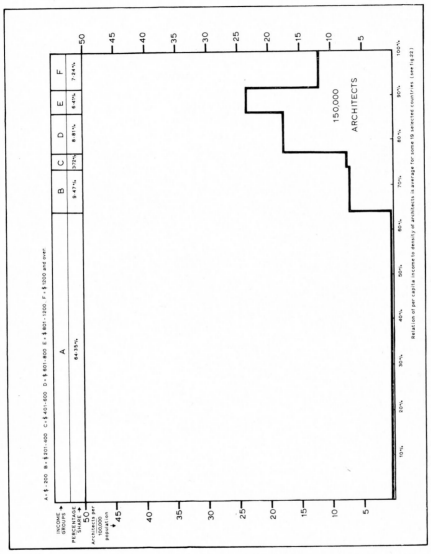

Fig. 23. Distribution of world population according to per capita income and architects per 100,000 population. (Per capita income 1959—Architects 1958, 1959, 1960.)

Fig. 24. Architectural creation in the world today: out of a total of 20 per cent that may be influenced by architects, it is only perhaps 2 per cent of the total architectural creation that is completely controlled by them, although their numbers correspond up to 5 per cent of the total needs

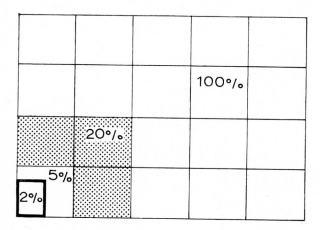

a percentage basis, it is the category which we could call natural architecture; that is, architecture as conceived by the inhabitants and the natural self-taught builders, the masons and the master masons.

The second category, which has appeared lately, is what the architects used to call 'architecture'; that is, architecture as a product of university training.

In between these two we have hybrid solutions of many kinds, solutions which are quite unenviable since they are the misinterpretations of an architecture which is itself very often a misinterpretation of what architecture should be (see Fig. 12, page 51).

If we now try to look at the qualitative influence of architecture we shall recognize that:

First, architecture as conceived by architects is so limited quantitatively that it has no significant qualitative influence over the total creation.

Second, even where it is of high quality, the creation is very often limited to a single building which loses enormously by its

Fig. 25.   The architect's influence in space: an example of
an area of great influence

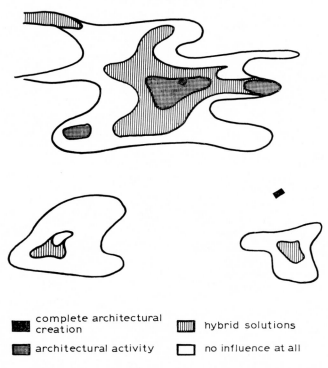

| | complete architectural creation | | hybrid solutions |
| | architectural activity | | no influence at all |

connection with the surroundings. Thus a building which alone
might have increased the importance of architecture will be lost
within unimportant surroundings. We must always remember
that architecture cannot be limited to the building itself, but must
radiate to its surroundings.

Third, the quality of architecture is such that even its direct
product is questionable in many instances. Architects themselves
have not really decided in which direction they want to go.

Last, as architecture taught in schools, whether good or bad,
is spreading all over the world and mixing with another type
of architecture, that which I have called natural architecture,
hybrids are created. These confuse the situation enormously.

The conclusion is that, irrespective of the good quality of a small proportion of architecture, the overall result is that we have a very bad architectural output. Taking quantity and quality together, it is questionable whether in one millionth of our architecture today we are doing what should be done, or contributing at all towards a better architectural future.

THE ARCHITECT'S FAILURE

The previous statements about the influence of the architect on the number of the buildings which are created and the quality of the work done prove positively that the architect, as we understand the term today, has completely failed in his mission. We are certainly entitled to say this of a profession that has managed to influence only a very small part of the total activity in its field and managed to contribute so little to the creation of better living conditions for humanity. How can we justify our existence to the average man if he knows that we don't serve him either directly, as his house is not built by an architect, or even indirectly, as we don't contribute to the creation of a better habitat? These facts are inescapable and we can no longer continue to bury our heads in the sand.

Before carrying our argument any further, let me make clear why I speak so positively of the architect's failure. The reasons are as follows:

(a) In quantitative terms the architect is not in charge of more than 5 per cent of the total building activity all over the world, or more than a millionth of the total creation of urban space.
(b) In qualitative terms a very large part of even this limited activity is of very low quality either because of the forces of inertia or because of a misunderstanding of the architect's role.
(c) Worthwhile architectural achievement is limited to some few good buildings. These do not form public architectural space within the human settlements, however, and thus their effect is largely lost.

There are a very few single buildings which have managed to create new concepts of architecture and contribute to the creation of a better way of living and a very few groups of buildings where architectural space is created; but these are not sufficient to justify the activity of architects all over the world or the existence of the schools of architecture. Let us not forget that two of the three men commonly accepted as the greatest living architects (Le Corbusier, Mies van der Rohe and Gropius) did not study in schools of architecture and began to create architecture on their own initiative.

What all this leads to is a definition of the role and duties of the architect, as well as an examination of the role and meaning of architecture.

Is architecture limited to the designing of a few buildings, to presenting a good façade on a street and creating a few rationally shaped rooms inside? Can we be justified as architects if we create single buildings which are satisfactory by themselves? Is it enough for us to build them within the frame of such inadequate layouts and town plans that the net results do not contribute to the creation of a better environment, a better habitat as a whole, or is the meaning of architecture something richer? Could the meaning of architecture be simply to produce a few satisfactory buildings at some point in the cone of the total building activity of humanity, or is architecture supposed to do something more than that?

THE MEANING OF ARCHITECTURE

These last questions raise some basic problems concerning the very nature of architecture. What do we mean by architectural creation? And why do we speak of the influence or lack of influence of architecture, its being limited to a particular area or its producing hybrid solutions?

In speaking of architecture, we have all along assumed it to mean not so much the total building activity as a technique and an art taught in the universities—a product of the organized technology of developing countries. In this sense architecture has the limited influence which we have attributed to it.

But this was not always so; for architecture (from the Greek *architekton*, meaning 'master mason' or 'master builder') was essentially the art of building. As such, it was the expression of the best techniques available in a certain age, as well as the expression of those powerful minds which, through natural selection, found themselves at the top of the cone of architectural creation. The peak of this cone in every culture represented the monumental expression of the craft of building as exercised by every mason and builder throughout the country.

Today, in the era of rapid socialization and developing interest in the whole of humanity, architecture is not justified in concentrating on one or a few exceptional buildings or groups of buildings, but should be able to cover a community, a region, a country; in short the total building activity all over the earth.

This interpretation is due not only to the broader social concepts of our era, but also to the fact that it is no longer possible to differentiate between the important and the unimportant parts of a city or between its monumental and non-monumental sections; for cities today are characterized by an all-inclusive conception of architectural space.

Thus, if we accept architecture as the technique and art of covering the total building activity, we will necessarily conclude that architecture is also enormously influenced by science, since in our time everything tends to become more and more scientific.

Looked at from a scientific standpoint, architecture is less advanced than any other field of activity in our era. Architectural research is very limited; moreover, there is very little work being done regarding the proper conception of architectural space inside and outside buildings or the relation of man to his living-space in terms of physiology, micro-climate or aesthetics.

Similarly, architecture lags behind in the field of constructional techniques, where its contribution is still elementary, not to say primitive, in contrast to the revolutionary achievements elsewhere. Finally, due to the great inertia of architectural creation, we can also state that architecture is lagging behind from the point of view of art too.

This proper conception of architecture as covering the total field of building activity reminds us of the way in which architecture was created. It was really created at the bottom level of the cone of total building activity, then gradually refined as it went to a higher level, until at length it found its monumental (though not necessarily the best) expression at the top of the cone.

Architecture could in this way be called the total building activity with its monumental expression at the top. Thus several people in several eras took the top of the pyramid as a whole and defined that architecture as only the technique and art of monumental buildings.

It is during the last few generations only that the situation has changed, and that architecture has been directly created at the top. spreading from there to the lower levels. Thus, where architecture formerly expressed the high point of a craft being carried on throughout the world and was a natural product of the total building experience, it is now conceived and taught to people at a different level, and tries to influence the total activity from the top downwards (Fig. 26).

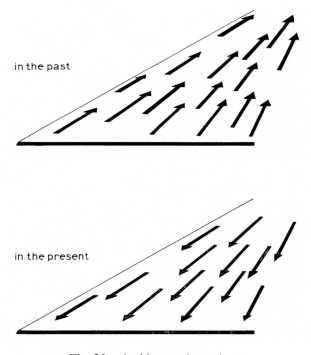

in the past

in the present

Fig. 26.   Architectural creation

Fig. 27.   Architectural creation in space in the past. Outgoing
forces were leading to expressions of higher order

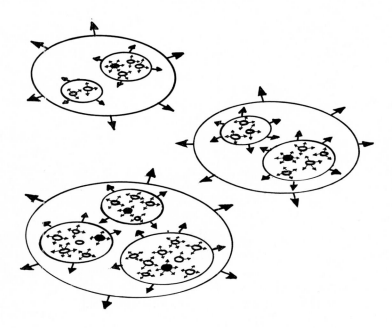

If we want to look at the same problem in space we shall have to
examine the forces which led to the creation of architecture and their
modes of operation. In the past, architectural creation in space moved
in one direction, from the smallest elements to the largest ones. A
peasant would build his hut, a mason would build a better house, a
better mason would refine this house, a master mason would build
the major buildings in every settlement and the best master masons
would create the monumental architecture. Monumental architecture
was not created at the top of the cone without direct relationship
to the smaller elements in space; in fact, the opposite is true, for
it was a product of architectural creation at the level of the nuclei or
cells which gradually assumed a monumental character at the top
through a process of selection (Fig. 27).

F

In the future, architectural creation in space is not going to work in the same way. On the contrary, it is going to move unilaterally. Instead of starting at the lowest level, from the smallest nuclei, and moving upwards, it will start at several centres of government, economy or education—and spread in all directions. For example, an industrial concern with its own research department will influence architecture immensely because of the products it creates. The government will influence architecture by defining through its national planning machinery not only economic standards for every house, but also all kinds of standards related to cost, production, physical aspects, etc. On the other hand, schools and centres of engineering will be able to influence construction methods through research and education, and these methods are going to have a very great impact on architecture. Meanwhile, schools of architecture will try to co-ordinate all efforts and bring them to a common focus. In this respect the task of the schools of architecture in the future is going to be much more complicated than it was in the past. It will be their duty to understand properly all tendencies of the political and social structure, the economy, the technique or the arts of a country, and express them in such a co-ordinated manner as will lead to the achievement of the best total architectural product (Fig. 28).

At present the situation is confused, since the picture of architectural creation consists of several forces coming out of the past, in addition to several forces of the future which are already in full development—and in some areas of the world perhaps even in full control. But because these future trends are still at an early stage of development, humanity has not managed to co-ordinate the findings of government, industry, engineering or art into a single coherent architectural expression. The diagrams presented in Figs. 27 and 28, if superimposed, will give us a very good picture of the architectural confusion we are in.

It becomes clear from these diagrams that in the future the problem of co-ordinating all forces of architectural creation towards an end-product of higher quality will become a very difficult and complicated task. It also becomes clear that if present trends continue we are going to have a transfer of radiation from the lowest level to a much higher one. This means not only that the influence of the

Fig. 28. Architectural creation in space in the future

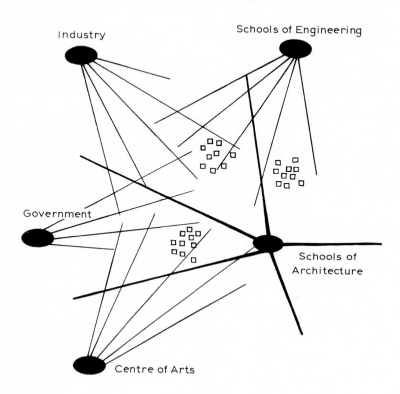

architecture which is created with every small hut or small building will cease to exist, but also that the influence of every kind of creation in every village or community of lower order is not going to be transferred upwards. There seems to be a danger in the field of architecture of a dictatorship springing up which will eliminate all forces having local importance. In fact, when architecture in the past was created at the lowest level, local conditions varied so much from one community to another that there was opportunity for a variety of architectural expressions at different levels, these being gradually screened out at higher levels by the survival of the best. As things are, this will no longer be possible in the future, and will consequently pose one of the major problems we shall have to face.

In fact, this tendency should be taken into consideration in combination with another, of which we have already spoken, the tendency to have more and more people participating in the creation of every single building. While in the past a single building was created solely by the mason responsible for it, we may in the future see in every single building the working together of many cultural, artistic and other influences, as well as the incorporation of products from many parts of the world in the creation of which many people have participated.

It is now high time to recognize that the failure of architecture coincides with the epoch during which architects are produced in a different way. Throughout the history of humanity, as far as we know, the architect was considered a natural leader not only because he was better than the others in his craft, but also because he was gradually selected as the best among the total number of people dedicated to building. In this way he was not the designer of buildings, but the leader of the building industry. He was not limited to a theoretical responsibility for his own product, but was directly related to its failure or success. He was at the same time the man who conceived, designed and built a building in a satisfactory way. He was equally concerned with the task of satisfying the needs of the inhabitants and that of providing them with a certain product at the lowest possible price.

Let us draw a comparison and assume that we are speaking of a motor-car factory. Are we going to call the chief architect of this factory the man who styles the cars, or the engineer who is concerned with the power of the engine? Or is the general manager of the factory more entitled to be called the chief architect of the new product because he is the one who co-ordinates all the activities from the conception to the realization and marketing of the car? I think that if we want good cars to satisfy our needs we should have to rely on the people who are responsible for every activity, from dreaming about new types of cars to seeing them off the production line into the supplier's and even the buyer's hands.

In this respect we must recognize that the beginning of the problems which we described as related to a transitional period in architecture coincides with the different meaning which we assign to the word 'architecture'.

Now, after recognizing the rising tide which is working against all of us, after assigning the architect's responsibility in this domain, after finding out how little his influence is and after explaining that the meaning of architecture is not confined to the creation of a few single buildings, much less to the design of them, we have reached the point at which we can define what the role of the architect must be.

The only way to get ourselves out of the present crisis is to try to redefine the role of the architect. We can then go on to work out the new solutions for the new problems which we are facing.

THE ARCHITECT'S DILEMMA

Let us now recapitulate the findings about our situation. Inevitably, the process of creation in architecture today is different from what it was in the past and thus creates different problems for the architect. He was once the product of an evolution. He had been drawn out of the strata lying below him in the cone of total creation by natural selection. He had only to look up, for the roots of his past were deep in the mass of the total building creation. Today, however, things are different. Now the architect appears at the top of the cone and has to look down. If he does not he gets no notion at all of his connection with the total cone of creation, a cone on which he sits as an alien element.

Contrasting present-day architects with the architects of the Greeks, the *architekton*, the Ma'mur Khans of the Moguls or the master builders of the Middle Ages, we may make two observations.

First, that the architect of today has been set right at the top, so that he must step down again if he wishes to exercise his influence; and, second, that he has been banished from the building site and so has lost contact with the actual construction. Once the architect was first a mason and then a master builder. Now he is named a master builder at a university, but must descend to become a mason.

Now we know where we stand. We are a different product, born in a difficult era, when humanity is facing more problems in architecture than at any time before. It is precisely at this critical moment, when we go forward with only an education and the influence of what was lying at the top of the cone, that we need roots, the best and deepest roots possible. Otherwise we may one day find ourselves with no underlying strength. We now have a body of architects practising a new, different type of architecture; but although it is several decades old, it is in fact a very young type of architecture in its very conception. At the same time we have now to conquer the world. We certainly have to ask ourselves to what extent we can do it.

What is the role of the modern architect in the face of the rising tide, and how can we solve his problems? Is he to remain at the top of the cone and from there try to influence the foundations? Must he remodel our cities, fighting a losing battle as he contemplates the angry sea of old construction around him and feels the waves of new construction buffeting him on all sides, or must he create something new? This big dilemma of ours itself gives rise to a further series of questions for which the architect must brace his mind. Where is our new creation to be born and grow; in urban or in rural areas, in the old countries or in the new? Is the creation of new capitals like Chandigarh, Brasilia or Islamabad, the new capital of Pakistan, or those of the African countries a mere coincidence which will have no influence on the future trends of a wider evolution?

Here we have the architect facing important problems and asking himself whether he is to face the total architectural creation, or sit at the top of the cone and try to influence it downwards; whether to turn his attention to the development of all types of buildings in order to face all our needs, or simply to design monuments. Is he going to become a scientist who recognizes the full extent of his problem, analyses it and defines a policy and a programme to face it? Or is he doomed to remain a designer who, in order to cover up his weaknesses, professes to be a mason when we speak of art and an artist when we speak of construction? Is he going to mingle with the common man, even if he has to be an anonymous worker, in order to emerge some day, remoulded as by fire? Or is he going to live in an ivory tower, selfishly designing monuments and disregarding the trends and the needs around him.

Now we can understand the real magnitude of the architect's dilemma. Exactly how he is going to answer it, and what road he is going to choose, will be decisive not only for his future but for his very survival.

5   new solutions for new problems

IT IS at this point that the architect must seek a way into the future. Is this way already visible? I think not, because as we have demonstrated there is such a multitude of new factors entering our lives that it is as yet too early to decide which way to go. What the architect can do is stand still for a moment and think seriously about his future, for the great problems around him find their echo in the equally great problems within him. He must adapt himself not only to the changing world, but also to the changing requirements of his profession, and even to the notion that he may be on the wrong course altogether and may have to alter it.

The architect must recognize the new needs and new trends, and find new ways of coping with his problems. Although the situation as already described may look desperate to the layman, it is not so really. After all, if we are able to create such a confusion we must be able to get out of it. In fact, looking around us we can see that some new solutions to the great problems hemming us in already exist. If we analyse these new solutions in relation to our needs, doing our best to understand what the new requirements in fact are, then we shall be better equipped for the future.

We have already spoken of the fresh forces which have entered the arena: economic, social, political, administrative, technological and aesthetic. Architecture is no longer a matter to be decided solely by the architect, but must be thought out in conjunction with many other people and co-ordinated with many other views. Nor is it any

88 ARCHITECTURE IN TRANSITION

longer sufficient to say that we can indeed create the best architecture, but that society does not understand it or that governments cannot finance it, so that it all remains stillborn, a vague cipher on paper. This is not architecture, but merely designing. Architecture exists only when it is implemented by actual building.

We live in a developing world, and the only justification for architecture is its connection with the overall evolution of society. For our purposes we may define this as the expression of all the forces which influence the creation of buildings, bearing in mind that the architect is conditioned by economic as well as by aesthetic, by social as well as by technical, by political as well as by cultural considerations.

If we view architecture as a part of the overall development taking place around us we shall understand how much it is conditioned by environmental factors, factors that must seriously be taken into account. We shall also understand how much it is conditioned by non-environmental factors, and shall seek to satisfy their demands too.

A NEW ROLE FOR ARCHITECTURE

It is now clear that the new role of architecture requires an understanding of the new dimensions of our problem and the complexity of the forces which have created the present situation, both of which factors will create even more difficult situations in the future.

If we try to define the problems which architecture is facing today we will find that they can be divided into two categories. The first comprises the problems which require an understanding of local environmental situations and the role of architecture as the consolidating and co-ordinating discipline. The second category consists of problems which are not connected with the environment and require action at a much higher level. The problems here are those which architecture faces in relation to industry, art, government and the other forces of modern expanding society. It is our task to define the role of architecture in both these fields.

Architecture must be co-ordinated geographically, that is, with its environment at the local level. The house we build must be co-ordinated with other houses, buildings, squares, open spaces and traffic, but it must also be co-ordinated at a broader level with other similar activities. If we think of materials, then we must think not locally, but nationally, perhaps even internationally, about the availability and economics of materials, about the labour force, and about the economics which are influencing our creation. All these aspects must be integrated with one another as well as with other aspects of our activities. We must find the proper solutions for schools, for houses, for all the many kinds of buildings and functions which constitute our total architecture. In the same way, co-ordination has to be achieved hierarchically, not only at the local, but at all levels: regional, national and sometimes even international. In this way we can view our achievement within the larger framework of the world at large to which it belongs (Fig. 29).

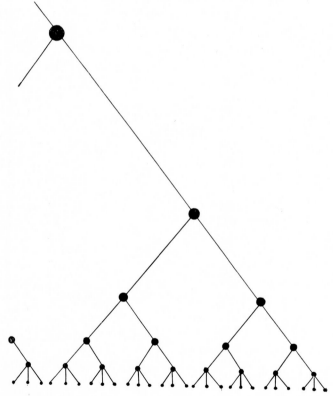

Fig. 29.   Architecture must be co-ordinated hierarchically at all levels, from the local to the international

Great achievements of the past, such as those cities, neighbour-hoods, communities and squares that we still admire as masterpieces of architecture, were certainly the result of the co-ordination of architecture at the local level first and then at higher levels.

It is easy to understand the necessity of co-ordination at the local level. What is more difficult, however, is to understand the necessity for co-ordinating architecture at higher levels, whether regional, national or even international, and the techniques by which this will be achieved. We have already seen that our present con-fusion is due, among other things, to the fact that architectural creation is influenced by forces derived from many unco-ordinated centres of radiation, such as industry, government, arts, engineering and architecture. We cannot continue our activity successfully unless we realize that schools of architecture, centres of architectural research and education, etc., must have the great task of co-ordinat-ing all forces influencing architecture, so that a total co-ordination radiating towards every area of architectural creation is finally achieved.

Architecture may now be seen in its proper context, as expanding in order to cover not only the centres of cities but the whole urban area, expanding into the countryside, flowing over into other coun-tries and not confining itself to the Western world alone. Architecture is to cover areas which still have buildings and ways of life of one, of ten or even more centuries, so that by expanding in space it acquires the real perspective of time, and is taught the rules of evolution.

A NEW ROLE FOR THE ARCHITECT

In this light the architect's role was and is that of a co-ordinator of several efforts. Within a house he is the co-ordinator of all needs and elements of solutions, whether economic, technical or social. He is to cover human needs with a physical shell which will probably have to be constructed of elements coming from many parts of the world and produced by other people. For many houses taken together, he is also the co-ordinator working for the creation of the neighbour-hood, which is to serve the needs not only of the family but also of the community. Moreover, he is to influence industry for the pro-duction of the best type of elements, use social sciences for the

Fig. 30. Architecture has to achieve local and spatial co-ordination, that is, cohesion between the elements and roots in their environment

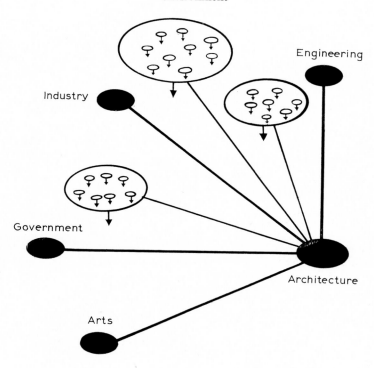

formation of a better human habitat at the level of the house or the level of the community and finally he has to urge and help governments to conceive proper housing policies.

Thus, we can call the role of the architect co-ordinator. He must create the necessary co-ordination at the highest level of architectural conception and implementation, as well as achieve local co-ordination, and spatial co-ordination, in the house and the small community; this is the living unit which is completely under the control of the architect and does not grow beyond him. This spatial co-ordination can now be expressed as a co-ordination of all architectural elements with one another, and as a co-ordination of all these elements with their surroundings. That is to say, architecture is going to seek the creation of proper spatial units and their proper relation to their surroundings. This implies cohesion between the elements and roots in their environment (Fig. 30).

Under present conditions of broader cultural spaces, however, the co-ordination has to be achieved simultaneously at the lower and higher levels, and we have to keep in mind the fact that these higher levels are much higher in relation to the past. In addition, the architect's role as a co-ordinator is much more difficult because the number of people and forces influencing the creation of even a single building have increased enormously, and can be expected to increase to an even greater extent in the future.

Let us first think of the number of people who influence the creation of one single building. In the past, in the very early stages of the evolution of human settlements, one man alone—the inhabitant of a hut—had to decide about its construction. The number gradually increased, but, so long as people relied on the skill and ideas of a local mason for the construction of their houses, the increase took place at a very slow rate. It was then the mason with the owner who had to decide about the shape of the house and its construction; and they were also the ones to decide about the local materials—the bricks, the timber and the tiles—that were to be selected and used.

Gradually, with the creation of broader cultural spaces, more and more people were involved in the decision-making until finally, in the last two generations, the number of people influencing the creation of a certain building increased at a much greater speed than in the past. It is now a fact that many decisions are involved in the construction of even the simplest of buildings. There is the government which will decide on the layouts of certain parts of the city and on related codes which have in turn been the product of innumerable decisions; there is industry which provides the materials for architectural creation, in the production of which many people have again been involved, and there is public opinion which exercises its influence on owner and architect alike. Thus, even if we take the case of a single building, we have now a much larger number of people exercising an influence on its creation and thus on the architect who is responsible for it.

But the situation becomes even more complex when not merely single buildings but whole communities are concerned, for the number of decision-makers is vastly increased. In the past, communities only reached a certain size, most often not exceeding a few tens of thousands of people. When communities increase in size and numbers, however, the number of people exercising an influence over them is also necessarily increased. In the past the community was formed either by one architect (rare though that was) or by natural evolution and growth from a few to a greater number of houses. Thus, the total number of people influencing the creation of the community could not exceed the total number of inhabitants of that community. In present-day communities, however, many other forces, such as the demands for through traffic, usually come into play. Thus we cannot avoid having the influence of the engineer, the traffic engineer, the traffic economist, the road designer or the road builder. In addition we have the forces of industry, born at and propagated from a different level, perhaps even from a different city, together with many other forces whose origin is not local. Thus, the community of the present, and much more the community of the future, is influenced by a much larger number of people than at any time before.

If we now look at the shell which is created in space because of the increasing number of people influencing the creation of a building and a community (Fig. 31), we shall see that it is a shell which was at first very small and is now increasing enormously in size. The architect who had to co-ordinate activities within that initial shell had his problem well under control; this is no longer so, however, for the total shell is expanding continuously and at an unprecedented speed.

The architect has thus a new and more difficult role, and unless he is to fail dismally he must play it more systematically than ever before. To do this he must understand exactly the nature and the dimensions of his role as well as the means he is going to use in playing it.

It is absolutely essential that architects should answer these questions concretely. The role of the architect is to create the best possible human habitat by co-ordinating conception, design and building in one harmonious whole.

How far, then, is the architect going to carry his role? When we speak of a community, or of the habitat in general, do we mean the total human community, on this earth, or do we mean the community as limited to a nation, a region or a broader metropolitan area? The community which is dealt with by the architect and for which he has

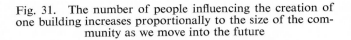
Fig. 31. The number of people influencing the creation of one building increases proportionally to the size of the community as we move into the future

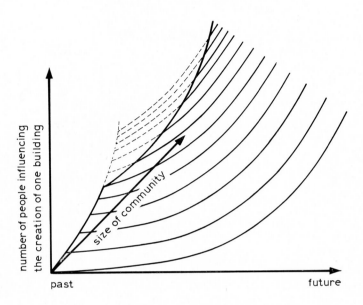

full responsibility is the human community, the community within which the human factor is of greater importance than the factor of the machine. Where the machine, whether a car, a train, a ship or an aeroplane, supersedes man himself, then other professions can play a greater role than the architect in the solutions to be given. The areas where this will occur should be communities of higher order. The architect will have to be:

(a) The co-ordinator for the formation of the habitat from the single building to the human community, as already described.
(b) The contributor of his architectural experience even to the formation of communities of higher order.

We can now define the extent of the responsibilities of the architect in space. In buildings and communities of lower order he is the co-ordinator of all other activities and of all other specialities— scientific, technical or artistic. He is the one to give the final shape to buildings and communities of minor order, the conception of which may be due to him or to people working at a higher level, be it at the level of the owner or client, or at the level of social, political and other sciences.

For communities of higher order the architect is the consultant who will be responsible for solving the problems of the physical formation of space so that these communities:

(a) Achieve full co-ordination with the communities of minor order for which the architect is responsible; and
(b) Reach a state that guarantees the best architectural expression.

What means is the architect going to use in order to achieve his goals? Will he work with the architectural knowledge of the past or is he going to use new means? The answer is definitely the latter. He will have to find new solutions to his new problems. He will have to understand first that his expanding subject has created the need for an overall view which it is beyond his ability to comprehend. This is the view of the general problems of human settlements, problems which are gradually becoming much larger in size and complexity. In order to cope with them he will have to follow the new approach of ekistics—the science of human settlements.

In order to create his buildings in the proper frame, he will have to understand the new types of urban settlements which are developing dynamically. In order to acquire a unit for which he will be responsible, he will have to recognize the human sector as the unit of his work. He will have to follow the proper solutions for houses and buildings and construction. Finally, he will have to understand that the synthesis can no longer be two-dimensional or three-dimensional, but will necessarily have to become a four-dimensional one.

The conclusions are quite simple. In order to play his new role, the architect has to:

(a) Resume his traditional role of master builder, as co-ordinator of all forces leading to the creation of the building, without limiting himself to the designing aspect of the creation.

(b) Expand his subject in size, so as not to include any longer just simple buildings but units which will better serve the new demands of his role; as well as to achieve architectural synthesis in the broader spaces created in the new type of expanding human settlements.

(c) Enter industry, government and centres of research and education where new notions about ways of living, the art of living, construction and the needs of production are being developed. In this manner architectural creation will be influenced at a new level. It is a level with which the architect is not yet acquainted but one with which he must familiarize himself if he is to achieve his purposes; and

(d) Proceed to all these activities in full knowledge that he is the scientist, the technician and the artist who is responsible for architectural creation. In order to achieve this he has to gain a much broader education than at present.

Only if he follows up the previous four points and enters every position influencing architectural creation will the architect be able to lead humanity towards a new architecture.

A NEW APPROACH: EKISTICS

Ekistics (from *oikos*, the ancient Greek word for a house or dwelling) is the science of human settlements. It co-ordinates economics, social sciences, political and administrative sciences, technology and aesthetics into a coherent whole and leads to the creation of a new type of human habitat. To work on such a habitat, the architect must now enrich his knowledge so as to be able to cover the related fields and co-operate with the community developer, the urbanist, the planner, the economist, the geographer and the social scientist, as a member of a single team. He has the chance of either guiding this team as its master co-ordinator up to a certain magnitude of subject, or of being merely the man who executes decisions about his work, decisions which are very often conflicting and in any case taken at different levels.

One might ask why architecture needs to turn to ekistics in our age, and why this was not necessary before. The answer is that the architect is forced to possess much greater knowledge and much greater ability if he is to cope with the rising tide of problems today. Evolution was so slow in the past that ordinary men were able to adapt themselves to the changing requirements of their age. Thus, to express the monumental architecture of his age, the architect—who was the master builder—could gradually create solutions and forms within a normal process of development. He had learned over a whole lifetime the ekistic requirements of his age. Such a situation is no longer possible, for in our world a single lifetime is not long enough to give us the experience we would require to emerge from mason into city-builder. We are therefore obliged to learn ekistics in order to be able to understand our problems, to grapple with them and with the changes which are taking place continuously.

An example will help us understand the expansion of the subject in one dimension at least, the dimension of space. In the past, even at his greatest, the architect was confined within the limits of a single community which coincided with the single small city, beyond which his interest did not need to go. The only case we know of a plan reaching beyond the limits of a city is that of classical Athens, which was physically connected with its port of Piraeus by means of the 'long walls'. This action, which was dictated by reasons of security, is the only case we know of planned building activity extending beyond the limits of a small urban community.

Today the pressure of people and economy on space is such that building activity has to be co-ordinated in ever-larger areas. This is true not only of the urban megalopolitan areas, but also of the rural areas, which in fact have become a synthesis of interwoven urban and rural functions. The example of a regional plan in Iraq, which led to the creation of new types of villages, and the comparison of this plan which has been made with calicospheriles or concretions of calcium carbonate deposited in the white of egg, proves how we have gradually had to face different types of problems and how architectural conception has to become a part of the broader study of human settlements which is the subject-matter of ekistics (Fig. 32).

Moreover, ekistics was not necessary in the past because architecture was growing naturally, and architectural creation extended only to limited physical sizes. Now architectural creation is growing physically at such a rate that it has gone beyond the control of the

G

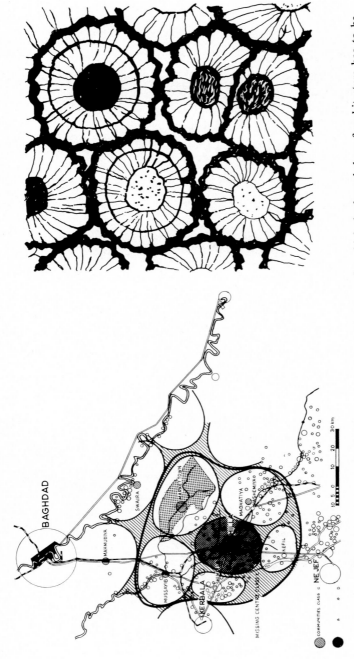

Fig. 32. Today we move towards the formation of broader spaces for which the knowledge of architecture has to be complemented by the knowledge of ekistics. A regional plan (Doxiadis Associates) for Greater Mussayib in Iraq has greater resemblance to a natural phenomenon (concretions of calcium carbonate) than to a product of architecture

architect; this makes necessary a different, more comprehensive approach, which is gradually moving from the status of a technique and an art towards that of a science. At present, total architectural activity is not growing in a natural way, but is created from the top. As such it has to be conceived and directed by ekistics, the science which illuminates problems of human settlements and defines the way which architecture and its fellow-disciplines must go.

A NEW FRAME: DYNAPOLIS

We can now turn our attention to the physical frame within which we place our architecture. Architecture today is mainly created within the broader urban areas. This will become more and more the case as the movement of the majority of the population towards the urban areas continues to increase, with the resultant decline in rural population. And as economic development forces more and more people out of the countryside towards the large urban centres, architectural activity is also leaving the rural areas. It is in the urban environment that we must look for the broader frame of our architectural creation of the present, and more especially of the future.

In the past, and up to the last two centuries, the urban areas were composed of small communities of not more than a few hundred thousand, more often with less than a hundred thousand inhabitants. These areas were not expanding to any important degree and seemed to their inhabitants to be static physical expressions which had conquered the two dimensions represented by the length and breadth of their cities. The situation has, however, changed within the last centuries. The static cities of the past, quite often surrounded by walls, have burst through their barriers and spread out into the countryside (Fig. 33). It was from that time on that the cities have grown continuously and have also conquered the third dimension, that of height, by expanding into multi-storey constructions.

In recent generations the growth of cities has taken place at such an unprecedented speed that the fourth dimension, the intangible dimension of time, has gradually become more important than the three physical dimensions. In this sense our cities have become four-dimensional, they have become dynamic. It is our lack of under-

Fig. 33.   The static city of the past has now burst its walls and spread into the countryside

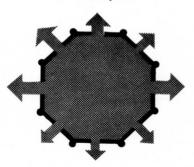

standing of this important transformation that is responsible for many of the problems of city planning and architecture today.

A little thought, even the most casual glance at the contemporary city, will prove the absurdity of what we allow to happen inside it, especially at its centre. Where the need is for large streets for heavy traffic, we have the narrowest streets; where we need big parking spaces outside public buildings we find the smallest parking facilities; where we need large plots for private and public functions there are very small and irregular plots; where we need freedom for new designs and new requirements there is no room to move at all; and where we need to expropriate and to change functions and facilities we have the largest investment and a premium on land values (Fig. 34).

We must conclude that the framework within which we create our architecture is wrong, binding its most basic precept thus. We must be on the wrong track. We must find a new conception of the city. What we need is not a static city, the limiting forces of which we have just demonstrated, but the dynamic city—dynapolis. This is the city of the future, conceived as a city which can expand and always be ready to create a new centre and new neighbourhoods.

It can now be clearly seen that within this city of the future there are two functions to be served: first, there are the functions which serve the entire city and are constantly expanding. These we will call central, whether or not they are actually at its centre. Secondly, there are the functions which we may call peripheral; that is, those pertaining to individual buildings or groups of buildings.

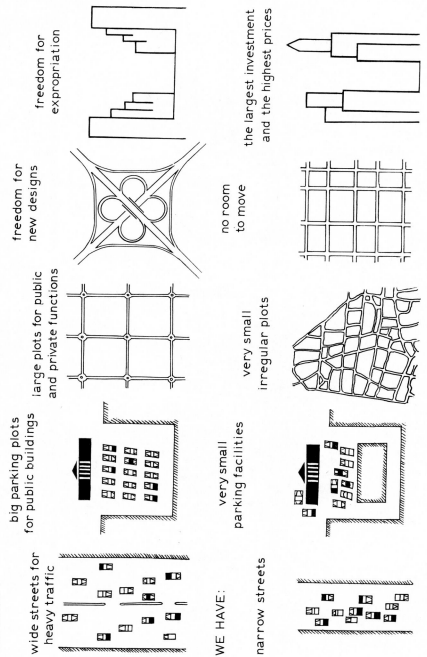

WE NEED:

wide streets for heavy traffic

big parking plots for public buildings

large plots for public and private functions

freedom for new designs

freedom for expropriation

WE HAVE:

narrow streets

very small parking facilities

very small irregular plots

no room to move

the largest investment and the highest prices

Fig. 34. The failure of city centres

Fig. 35.   From static to dynamic cities: the expansion in one direction
allows the centre to expand without difficulty

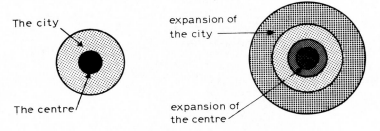

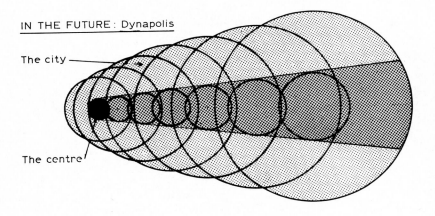

The city of the past was composed of two parts. It had its centre, and it had its periphery, which was mainly used for residential purposes. During the past two generations, however, due to the continuous expansion of the city, the centre has spread into the built-up area of the periphery, altering its structure and creating a variety of difficult or insoluble problems. The concentric expansion of our city has strangled its centre because it has left no room for expansion.

To avoid this it seems essential for city growth to be controlled so that the modern metropolis can expand only in one direction. It is only through such an arrangement that the centre and the periphery will remain in constant balance while the city expands to as yet untouched or uninhabited spaces.

Dynapolis will not be strangled to death, but will expand parabolically (Fig. 35) and will gradually take a geometric shape on the basis of a rectilinear system of axes (Fig. 36).

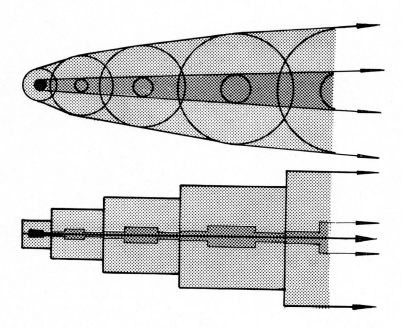

Fig. 36. The parabolic dynapolis will take rectilinear forms

The idea of dynapolis has not merely remained in the head of the theorist but has actually reached the stage of implementation in several cases, of which we mention two characteristic ones. The first of these is that of Khartoum, Sudan, where we see the principle of dynapolis applied to an existing city (Fig. 37). The second is that of Islamabad, the new capital of Pakistan, where dynapolis is applied to a new city (Fig. 38).

Another example of how the principles of dynapolis can

Fig. 37.   Khartoum: from three old cities towards a new dynapolis
(Doxiadis Associates)

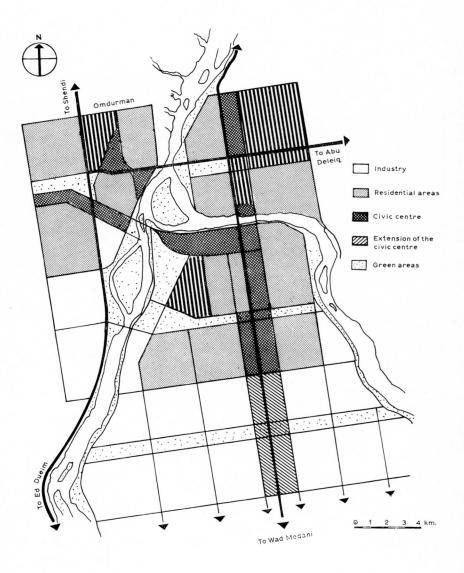

Fig. 38. Islamabad, the new capital of Pakistan: a new dynapolis
(Doxiadis Associates)

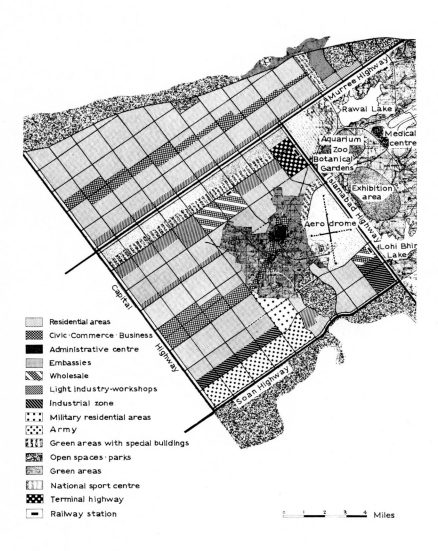

influence existing cities is the case of Washington, D.C., where the expansion of the city southwards along the Potomac River will relieve its heart of a multitude of pressures which have been accumulating over a long period of time and would in the end have killed it, as with every other city (Fig. 39).

Yet to say that we have set up the general framework of our architecture by placing it first in a rational context and now within the physical frame of dynapolis itself, does not answer our specific problems. We have already seen that architecture must now be created within a framework controlled by four masters: man, the car, the aeroplane and the rocket. We have also seen that it must be created within an expanding city. Now another question arises. How are we to set up the specific frame for every single building to be built? In order to answer this question we have to go beyond the general notions of ekistics and beyond the general frame of dynapolis and descend, so to say, to the 'grass roots', to the unit which must physically define architecture. This unit is the human sector, which is the basic element of the broader urban areas seen as a whole and the largest unit within which architecture remains in direct relation to man without the interference of the machine.

A NEW UNIT: THE HUMAN SECTOR

The concept of the human sector is born out of the fact that urban settlements of the present no longer have one master, but four: i.e. man, car, aeroplane and rocket. Under these circumstances, we have to recognize the necessity of preserving the first master as the one controlling the whole synthesis of the city. This is not possible over extended areas. Man on foot cannot cover distances much greater than two miles and even such a distance is probably too great.

We have therefore to reconcile ourselves to the idea that we must preserve the human scale so far as distances are concerned. These distances may be half a mile, one mile or a mile and a half. In very exceptional conditions they could be greater than that, but they could certainly not exceed two miles. If we assume that urban dwellers could, under proper conditions, walk for up to thirty minutes in order to go to their jobs, their theatres, their markets, etc., then this distance of a mile and a half appears to be the maximum distance

Fig. 39. The future extension of Washington, D.C.: one directional growth as an alternative to death by self-strangulation: C. A. Doxiadis's proposal to the Redevelopment Land Agency of Washington, D.C., in 1958

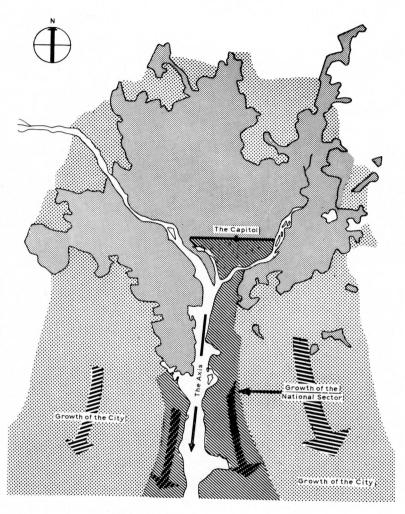

which can be allowed for a sector under the full control of man. Its ideal shape would seem to be an oblong, from half a mile to a mile in maximum length, so that people need walk no more than a distance of up to half a mile inside it to reach their schools, shopping areas, small parks and cultural and social centres, as well as other basic requirements of their neighbourhood or community.

How can the sector be under the full control of man if we allow that the car also has to serve man within that sector? The answer is a design allowing cars to enter any part of the sector and serve it, but without actually crossing it. Thus, the heart of the sector will be exclusively for pedestrians. The cars will run outside the sector at much higher speeds and inside the sector at ever-reduced speeds (Fig. 40).

It is now clear that the creation of a human sector was not necessary in the past because the whole community, the whole settlement, was on a human scale. Now, the creation of a human sector seems to be an absolute necessity for the reform of our cities. Old urban settlements, divided into blocks as they were, must now be redesigned on the basis of the new modulus, that of the sector (Fig. 41). The problem of how these sectors are to be rationally organized in the case of a large metropolis or megalopolis is a matter of special study which falls within the field of the structure of a dynamic city and cannot be examined in detail in the context of the present study.

We should be concerned here only with the buildings within a sector. There are some exceptions, however, in the case of settlements where some buildings will cross from one sector to the other like bridges, just as the bridges of Italian cities of the Renaissance passed over old canals or rivers. Similar bridges can be built between sectors which will contain the shops and other facilities necessary to attract people to move undisturbed from one sector to the other on foot (Fig. 42).

The organization of a city into sectors is, of course, not purely an architect's job; but the architect can certainly contribute, along with the traffic engineer, the economist or the urban geographer, to the understanding of the nature of the landscape, the synthesis of the city's one-directional axis, etc. It is within the sector, however, that the architect can create the proper architectural space and devise the proper architectural synthesis. And it is within the sector that we have to deal with the aesthetics not of the machine but of man. The machine—the car—will be confined to the highways where it belongs. What is more, we should not erect imposing buildings along our highways. where they can attract the attention of drivers. We should

Fig. 40a. A representative human sector built in Western Baghdad
(Doxiadis Associates)

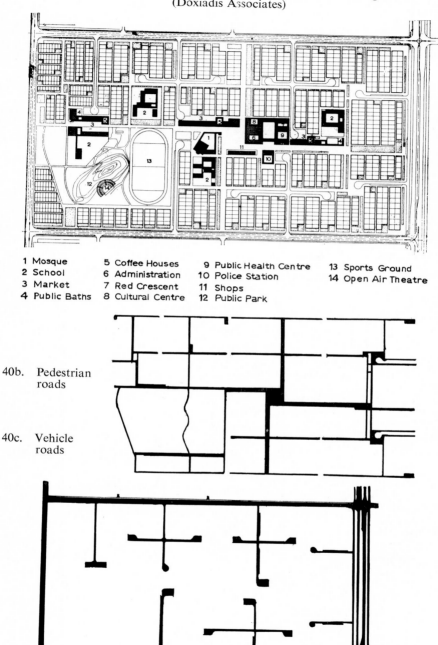

1 Mosque
2 School
3 Market
4 Public Baths

5 Coffee Houses
6 Administration
7 Red Crescent
8 Cultural Centre

9 Public Health Centre
10 Police Station
11 Shops
12 Public Park

13 Sports Ground
14 Open Air Theatre

40b. Pedestrian
roads

40c. Vehicle
roads

Fig. 41.   The modulus in the new city should be the sector instead of
the block

The Old City : here the modulus is the block

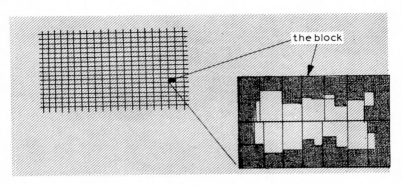

The New City in the Same Scale: now the modulus should be
the sector

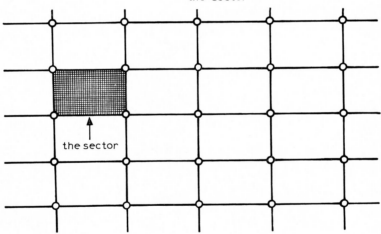

not erect any monument of the old type on a highway at all, because
not only can it not be seen properly by a driver speeding along at
sixty or eighty miles an hour, but it may even divert his attention and
so cause an accident. The important thing for a highway is for it to
have as clean a design as possible so that people can drive along it as

easily as possible. It should give an impression of neatness and balance of forms and colours and natural levels of landscape, but that is all.

In the human sector, on the contrary, where people walk, the values of architecture remain the old ones. An architectural scale exists within the house. This can be interconnected with the architectural space outside it in the courtyard, and this again with the architectural space of the street, of the small or major square or even of the park.

How this principle can be implemented may be shown for a variety of sectors, such as that in Baghdad (Fig. 43) and that in Eastwick (Fig. 44), or by the details of space included between rows of houses in the form of roads, squares, etc. (Fig. 45).

The human sector must be conceived as a unit and as the shell of a growing organism of the future. It will need to be as self-contained as possible, with centralized functions, institutions and facilities, and possessing its own transport system. It may even one day be covered in, so that its houses and buildings are protected from the elements. Such sectors have already been and are being built in several countries for several types of communities and their existence is becoming more and more necessary every day.

These human sectors are going to replace the antiquated city block and become the shell of the city of the future. Only in them can we create a proper framework for our architecture, which is otherwise going to be lost for ever in a sea of cars.

Such sectors will have to be designed to meet a large variety of problems. They may some day need to become the framework for the creation of a radically different type of architecture in a different synthesis, but they will always have to remain human sectors, for it is only in such a way that we can achieve a greater synthesis, merging into broader and broader areas, until we have at last fulfilled the need of dynapolis, and our city grows into a dyna-metropolis and beyond it.

Here I want to reiterate my belief that it is only through such a gradual process of building up of sectors that we can ever create the city of the future. I firmly believe that we cannot reverse the natural creation and expansion of a city and, for example, have our cars speeding along over the roof-tops as has been proposed by several

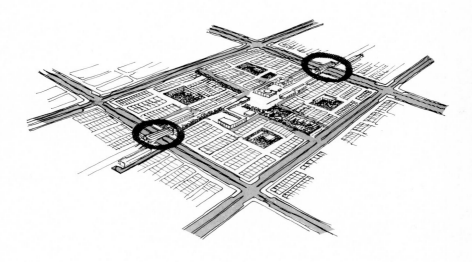

Fig. 42. Bridges between sectors in the centre of the new port town of Tema in Ghana. The bridge for pedestrians is an extension of the architecture of sectors with shops on both sides (Doxiadis Associates)

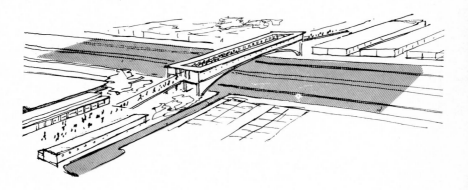

people, for this would seem to me a solution for the city not of the future but of the past.

The human sector must be very carefully designed in order to create the proper conception, the proper size of space in every part of it, even if we occasionally have to reverse some recent ideas such as, for example, that streets should be very wide. Let us see how reasonable this is. They should certainly be wide if we have a large number of cars to drive along them. But if we don't have this large number of cars or if we want them not to pass between houses but rather to remain at certain distances from them, then the roads should have dimensions which are only human. Thus, such roads may be better from the point of view of micro-climate for hot areas and may create a much better feeling of community, in addition to being more economical in construction, maintenance, etc. Such are the roads we have designed in many schemes for Iraq and other hot countries. They are not merely more economical for the city and the inhabitants

Fig. 43. A human sector in Baghdad, Iraq. In the middle from bottom to top is the main axis of pedestrians with all central functions (Doxiadis Associates)

H

Fig. 44.   One of the many human sectors in the large Eastwick project,
Philadelphia, Pennsylvania (Doxiadis Associates)

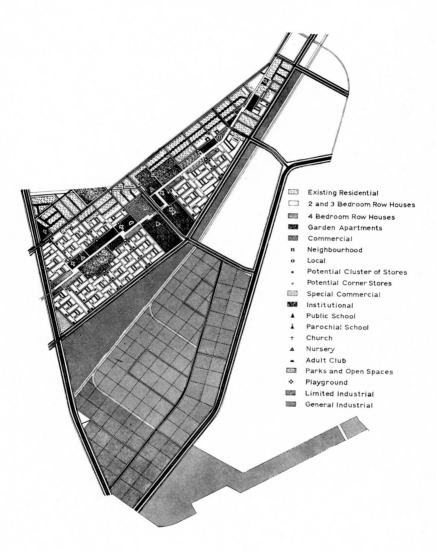

Existing Residential
2 and 3 Bedroom Row Houses
4 Bedroom Row Houses
Garden Apartments
Commercial

n   Neighbourhood
o   Local
•   Potential Cluster of Stores
∘   Potential Corner Stores

Special Commercial
Institutional

▲   Public School
ǂ   Parochial School
+   Church
△   Nursery
▬   Adult Club

Parks and Open Spaces
❖   Playground

Limited Industrial
General Industrial

and much better adjusted to the local conditions, but also create a much better space and enable people to feel as much at home in them as they do inside their own houses (Fig. 46). Making man feel at home everywhere in a city is one of the greatest obligations we have, especially if we want man to be and remain the master of his city.

THE HOUSE: A CHANGING ORGANISM

The main element inside most human communities is the house or the single family dwelling unit. How can we solve the problem of the house of the future? We must recognize from the very beginning that we shall have to find several different types of solutions. We have already explained the changing nature and content of the house, and if we want it to be properly adapted to our age we shall also have to understand that the very concept of the house itself is undergoing a change.

In rural areas or neighbourhoods of single houses and relatively low density, it is possible to provide each family with a plot which will suffice even if that family reaches its maximum size. In such cases we can follow the policy of making our houses grow and expand (Figs. 47 and 48). Such a policy, which was first used as the basis of the solution to the problem of rural rehousing in Greece, where 200,000 houses were constructed, was later used in other national housing programmes also (Fig. 49).

The necessity for a growing or expandable house may lead to any one of a number of courses of action: for example, in a city we might build the ground floor first and add the second floor later, or we might build a two-storey unit and only later add parts, such as rooms or minor auxiliary elements. This kind of idea will lead to a radically different design of house, one allowing for natural and gradual growth, to be followed perhaps by its redivision and re-allocation among more families, yet still providing for its final reunification into a single house if and when that proves necessary.

There are, of course, certain areas where such ideas could not be implemented, and we would then need to consider the co-operative house, within which a family can change or exchange units inside a broader complex of buildings, so that the family is always brought into a unit of appropriate size.

Fig. 45.   Detail of one of the sectors in Eastwick

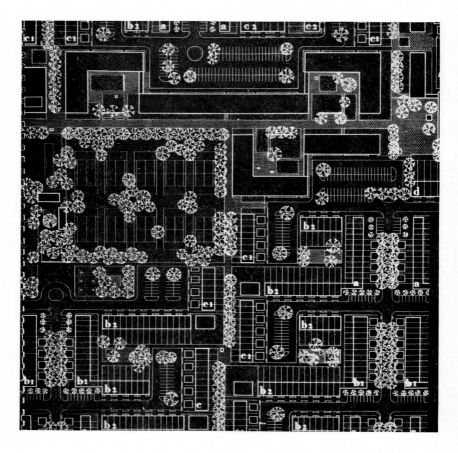

We have talked of growing and expanding houses, which are the result of the forces represented by changing family sizes and incomes. But other changes in technology and habits, which are also taking place, impose a change in the facilities provided by a house; and this is certainly possible if we conceive of a changing house where the basic frame is going to remain the same while internal partitions and fittings may be changed from time to time. Such a policy makes sense since the period of amortization of a structural frame can be much longer than that required for the finishing and furnishing of the house. Similarly, the frame of a human community—the highways around it,

Fig. 46. A road in Baghdad in human proportions (Doxiadis Associates)

community buildings and facilities within it—will last longer than its residential part. Thus the notion of growing, expandable and changing houses—which is basic for the future—fits into the conception of a changing (but not growing) human community. This applies also, though in a different context, to rented houses, where the change of size takes place according to the rules of a liberal economy. In all these cases the very conception of housing has radically changed.

Thus the necessity for the creation of broader groups of houses, where people will be able to move from a small unit to a large one and vice versa, now becomes especially apparent. These groups or units will gradually increase in size to reach a thousand or more houses, depending on the trend in the size of families and the corresponding desire for change in the size of dwelling. In this way we are led to the concept of a community built on the basis of a unified plan which will take us to the creation of communities of a size approximate to that of the human community. Reasons of economy in the use of developed land, among others, make it necessary to establish the human community as the modulus for the city of the future.

In developing such a system of ideas we have to bear in mind that, in countries of low incomes and in the early phases of development, the average family is larger than in the more-developed countries. This means that in less-developed countries we will have a larger variety of house-sizes than in the more-developed ones. If we now also take into consideration the increasing rate of socialization, which acts as an equalizer of income between families in developed societies, we shall find that there is also another reason why there will be less variation in the sizes of houses in a developing world.

These trends indicate that there will be less differentiation in the whole scale of house-sizes in the future than at present, and much

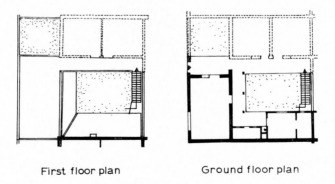

First floor plan   Ground floor plan

Fig. 47.   A growing urban house in Iraq
(Doxiadis Associates)

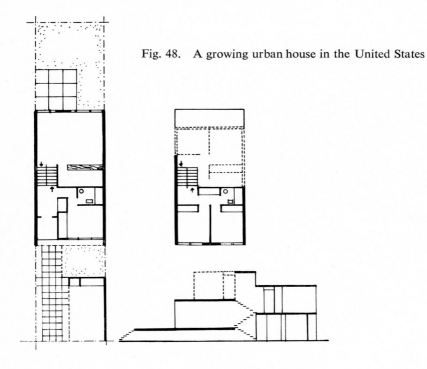

Fig. 48. A growing urban house in the United States

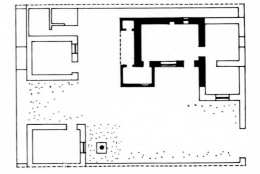

Fig. 49. A growing rural house in Greece: one of the many types of growing houses used for the reconstruction of Greek villages between 1947 and 1951. The nucleus of the house (in black) was built by the Government. The white parts have been gradually added by the owners

less than in the past. Such tendencies may lead to general non-owner-ship of houses or dwellings. On the other hand they might, because of increasing incomes together with decreasing differences between sizes of houses, as easily lead to the ownership of a house by every family throughout its entire life. What the general outcome for humanity will be in this respect is at present unknown, for it will depend mainly on the development of new cultural patterns and the desires of the majority of the people. One thing is certain, however, that, regardless of the conditions of ownership in the houses of the future, it seems imperative to form houses into broader groups, in order to:

(a) create a human scale between them,
(b) serve them best by machines and cars, and
(c) have the proper balance of all types of families within the same area, so as to allow all types of policy in ownership and avoid segregating certain types of families.

BUILDINGS: A FRESH VIEW

As against the residential units of houses, dwellings and flats, we have the broad category of all other buildings. With them, too, there are several possible cases. We may have buildings which need expansion; this is what usually happens, for example, when we start a school, a college, a factory or a hospital.

Buildings start at a certain size but very soon have additional needs; either because of an expansion of the same needs through an increase in the number of people served by the building, or because the same people develop new kinds of needs. A school, for instance, may acquire either a larger number of children or additional needs for laboratories. We must therefore plan our buildings so as to allow for growth of all kinds, and a different approach to the notion of synthesis is thus forced on our minds. This, together with the necessity for handling so many building projects with the small task force of architects at our disposal, compels us first to design such buildings with standardized elements, a standardization not only of material but even of whole segments of classrooms, laboratories, etc., and to proceed only then to a synthesis according to the requirements of each specific case (Fig. 50).

Fig. 50.   Different school buildings in Iraq built with standardized elements of
one or two classrooms and auxiliary spaces (Doxiadis Associates)

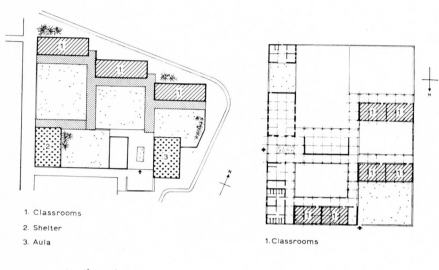

1. Classrooms

2. Shelter

3. Aula

1. Classrooms

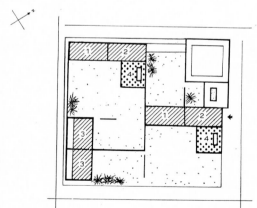

1. Two classroom wing - Two storeys

2. One classroom wing and stairs - Two storeys

3. Gymnastic shelter

4. Auxiliary spaces

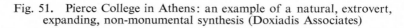

Fig. 51.   Pierce College in Athens: an example of a natural, extrovert, expanding, non-monumental synthesis (Doxiadis Associates)

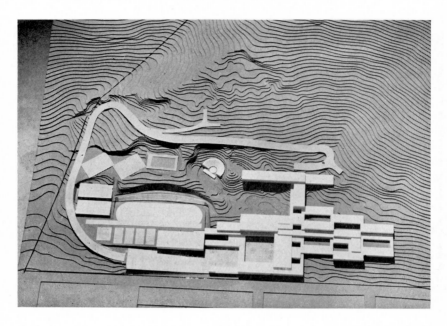

Such ideas lead to an expanding synthesis. They result in much more rational and logical building complexes, which are extrovert and not monumental or introvert and so necessarily static (Fig. 51).

This synthesis should be based on interconnected buildings. It could be said, certainly, that we should always plan our buildings separately and within the same compound or enclosure. But this does not usually give us a synthesis, since it creates negative space and wasted movement. It is only when we bring our buildings very close together and then make them expand as one building complex that we can be sure of an appropriate synthesis.

In this way we shall achieve not only positive buildings but also positive syntheses of buildings, by the creation of open spaces having positive and not negative character. We return basically to the idea of buildings grouped around certain open spaces, spaces which are interconnected and themselves become part of the synthesis (Figs. 52, 53). This centuries-old principle is a very sound one, and was lost only because architects tended to take an academic interest in the external appearance of their buildings, and not in the creation of positive architectural space.

On the basis of the principles we have outlined we can create even larger syntheses, like that of the University of Panjab, where a human sector has been created which started from a core and expanded in all directions, while keeping the hierarchy of functions and retaining all the potential of a living organism for expansion within the synthesis (Figs. 54, 55, 56, 57).

Fig. 52. The central courtyard of the Doxiadis Associates headquarters in Athens: an open space in the centre turns into an integral part of the building. It is architectural space

The important thing is that the synthesis must be free, non-symmetrical and non-academic, so that we can develop our notions freely and let our architecture expand. On these principles we can definitely create major syntheses; with the human sector, the growing building, the expanding and changing house, we serve the needs of socialization and greater production so that architecture can again venture to appear in our cities in the form of major projects.

Projects now envisaged in some countries for the centres of their major cities aim to serve just such a purpose. Architecture, lost because of the small scale of its subject in relation to the enormous scale of human creation, is once more beginning to gain in importance (Fig. 58).

But these ideas of growth which are the basis of our synthesis must not lead us to think that the only possible solutions are extrovert solutions of growth, and that we may not also retain our introvert ones. On the contrary, our introvert buildings now assume a far greater importance on the frame of a human community, for we can now see them more closely and study them as monuments. Besides being a symbol, a monument also serves certain needs. But it should not require expansion or then it is not a monument. With this characteristic in mind, we can and must study the monument as an introvert building in its own right (Fig. 59).

Fig. 53.   Interconnected open spaces: a market-place in Western Baghdad composed of a group of internal squares with all types of central community functions. See also layout in Fig. 43 (Doxiadis Associates)

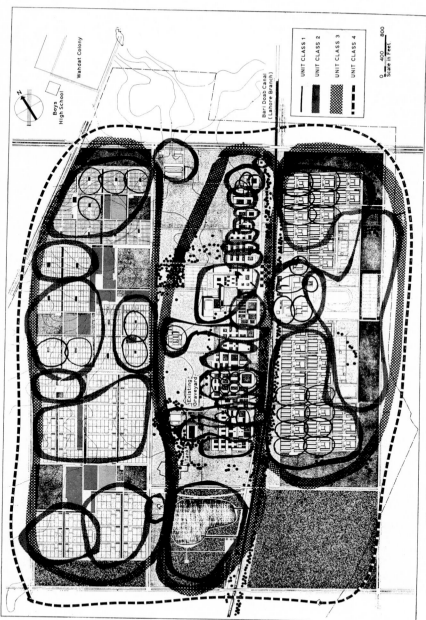

Fig. 54. The University of Panjab as a human community (Doxiadis Associates)

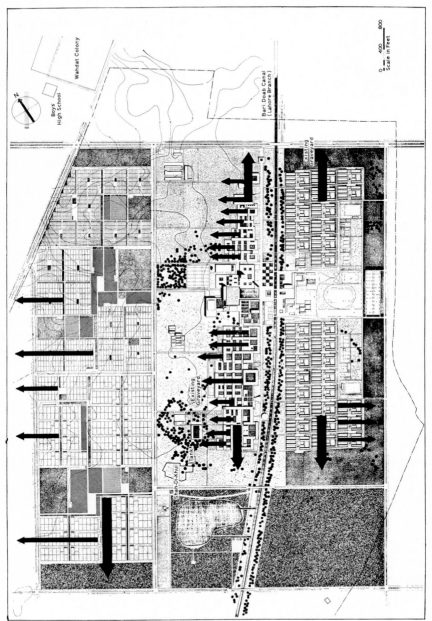

Fig. 55.   The University of Panjab as an expanding synthesis

Fig. 56.　The University of Panjab as a synthesis of positive spaces

Fig. 57.   The University of Panjab: the main axis of the synthesis is not abstract
and symmetrical but a corridor connecting all buildings and courtyards

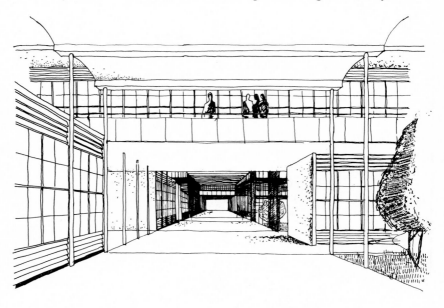

So we see that architecture can express the life within itself by
growing always from the inside towards the outside. Rodin spoke of
the internal forces conditioning the surface of his sculpture, a surface
which only covered the forces within it; in the same way architecture
must have as simple as possible a skin, conditioned by the life within
it.

Buildings can and should follow the same rules as those applying
to houses; they should not only consist of standardized parts but
should be expandable and changing. This is indispensable for some
and necessary for all, especially within the changing parts of dynapolis.
Thus we are led to the notion of a structural frame which can serve
many types of changing and different functions at different periods
in the life of the building. This means the development of all-purpose
frames to be used as the basis for buildings of changing functions;
subsequently, this will lead to the necessity for imaginative but all-
purpose syntheses, where the 'finish' could also give the building a
special character.

Fig. 58. One of the centres of a new community for half a million people in Korangi, a part of Karachi, Pakistan (Doxiadis Associates)

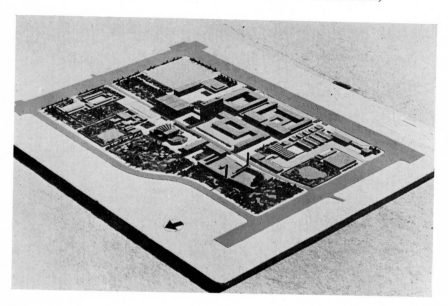

On the basis of the previous ideas, and by the creation of human sectors with an understanding of the new necessities of housing and the new necessities for buildings, we can always differentiate the various functions of the elements within our city or our sector, and provide the appropriate solutions for them. Housing and buildings must both follow the laws of an expanding synthesis of positive space and should be constructed on the basis of well-studied, standardized units. Monumental buildings can, on the contrary, be non-standardized and, in distinction to the others, detached and introvert.

BACK TO THE ESSENTIALS OF CONSTRUCTION

Standardized units are necessary for the creation of broader complexes of houses and buildings. Standardization, however, is not to be limited to types of houses or major parts of houses and other buildings, but must extend to the very elements of construction.

The need for standardization was always present in minor parts

I

Fig. 59.   The Cathedral of Axum: an introvert building with monumental
            importance (Doxiadis Associates)

Fig. 60.   A synthesis based on prefabricated marble slabs with different finishing
            on the floor and the walls (C. A. Doxiadis's home in Athens)

of construction, as for example in bricks and tiles, and there was always a tendency to build certain types of houses, schools, etc. In our era a changing economy and technology, as well as a greater demand for quality, make it more necessary than ever before to standardize all elements of construction which are amenable to pre-fabrication, and thus to less expensive production. Moreover, both these tendencies towards standardization, which start from the smallest parts of architectural creation (bricks) and the largest (house, school building units, etc.), necessarily lead towards a standardization of major constructional parts such as doors, windows, panels, walls and even complete rooms, multi-rooms, parts of buildings, etc.

The forces resulting in this phenomenon of overall standardization are many. Apart from economics and technology, it is a fact that we are changing over more and more from the heavy materials of the past to the new light materials, and it is equally true that wherever we make this change we seem to revert to a natural standardization. This has been happening in Japan for centuries, as well as in other countries which produce light materials for local types of construction, such as mats in Bengal, etc. Heavy materials did not lend themselves to such types of construction, but we are now entering an age during which new, light materials are gaining more and more ground.

But we must not imagine that this applies only to frameworks—that is, to timber and metal constructions. With bricks and concrete blocks, too, we can achieve a standardization which will allow for all kinds of solutions. The solutions given lately by a variety of concrete blocks is the best proof of the great possibilities which exist even with heavy materials. I have personally had occasion to try the results of such prefabrication even with marble slabs (Fig. 60).

Such prefabricated elements can serve many purposes and perhaps solve all our problems. We can use them to create either the skin of our building or its internal parts; we can make them take the weight of construction, or simply constitute its surfaces, inside and outside the buildings; we can even use them for our basic furniture (Fig. 61).

Now these notions of standardization inevitably lead us to the use of a modulus in all types of construction. As used by a person like me who looks on himself as a mason, such a modulus could be nothing but a modulus repeated in an arithmetical way. The best unit I could find for the creation of buildings on such a basis was a human unit

Fig. 61. Prefabricated wall containing cupboards, a bar, radiators, loud speakers, various shelves, etc. (C. A. Doxiadis's home in Athens)

derived from our footstep. This is what conditions our floors, which in turn condition the layout, and it is naturally expandable to the other dimensions of our buildings (Figs. 62, 63).

With this kind of a modulus we can create all types of buildings. We can even create furniture, adapting the basic furniture-wall to a variety of needs, with the exception only of furniture intended for seating and tables.

In case we imagine that prefabrication influences only the architect, or that it is a product only of the great industries of Western civilization, I should like to mention two examples which demonstrate that it is in fact a very human phenomenon influencing arts as well as construction in all parts of the world. A visit to the shop of a small craftsman producing statues of gods in India, or to the shop of another craftsman producing all types of window-frames and djallis in Pakistan, would convince us of the truth of this statement (Figs. 64, 65).

Fig. 62. Modulus in practice: a photo of the house of Fig. 63
(C. A. Doxiadis, Architect)

Standardization is an age-old demand which has now become imperative. With this in mind we can now conceive an architecture which is the total of a larger number of different combinations of a greater variety of standardized elements than ever before. This is true for all sizes of architectural creation, from complete buildings to structural elements. Not only are more and more of the latter going to be prefabricated, but the process will move to larger and larger units, progressing from the ready-made door to the ready-made house, or other minor type of building (Fig. 66).

Parallel to this trend we are going to witness a gradual elimination of many elements of which man was at first so proud that he enjoyed showing them off, but which are now beginning to be used in different, more modest ways. The discovery of electric lighting led first to large electric chandeliers but later to the incorporation of light bulbs into the ceiling. In the future we shall probably witness wall-panels producing light, a discovery which will eliminate difficulties, discomfort and will add to the aesthetic appearance of a room. Such trends are going to lead away from an architecture of fittings towards an architecture of space.

As a result, architecture tends to become a game in which the winner finds the best possible combination of a number of elements of increasing size. Thus, in one respect, the architect will become more and more the master mind whose synthetic ability will create the best possible shell, the best possible space to live in, utilising a number of given elements. Looking at this from a different angle, however, the architect can be the master mind in the production of these elements which will, in turn, create the best possible architecture. In the second instance he is the master mind of production, in the first he is the creator of living-space.

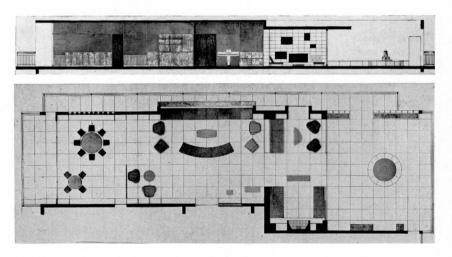

Fig. 63.   C. A. Doxiadis's home in Athens designed on the 75 cm. (one-step) modulus. Figures 60 and 61 are interiors of the same house

Fig. 64.   Indian gods

Fig. 65.   Djallis in Pakistan

A FOUR-DIMENSIONAL SYNTHESIS

We have clarified the principles of an architecture to come, as well as the new solutions we are finding, but there is one underlying problem which we have so far not considered. We have discussed the requirements of a growing population, of a new economy, of socialization, technology, changing techniques and changing patterns of transportation, and in so doing have demonstrated the existence of many elements.

Overall, however, we came to the conclusion that the major factor common to all the contributory elements was the rapidly changing rate of growth, which has imposed 'time' on us as a fourth dimension.

We have dealt with our solutions concerning time within the framework of national development programmes, time in dynapolis and time in the creation of our buildings and houses, by proposing a different approach to the question of architectural synthesis. But

Fig. 66. Houses designed for Eastwick, Philadelphia. They consist of pre-fabricated elements which can be assembled in different ways for the creation of a variety of solutions

what relation does this new dimension really bear to the aesthetics of our proposed synthesis? I think we must assert that time is the essential dimension if we are to have an architectural synthesis in any meaningful sense of the word. In architecture, time is expressed mainly as movement. If we stop at one point then we no longer have architecture but mere scenic design, a piece of theatre. The examples of the Acropolis of Athens and of Luxor in Egypt are sufficient to impress upon us the importance of the axis of movement (Figs. 67, 68, 69).

To feel architectural space or architecture in general requires movement. Thus, if we do not take time into consideration, time expressed as motion within a synthesis, then we simply do not have a synthesis but a façade; we may have painting but not architecture. In the great ages of architecture the notion that architecture implies a time-dimension was always felt, so that the result of the synthesis compelled man to walk through it, to feel and then become a part of a piece of architecture, and not merely remain outside it as an onlooker.

In the cases already mentioned of Egypt and Greece, man was compelled to walk through a whole complex of buildings and live within it in order to achieve his end. This was equally true in other great eras of architecture, as in the cases of the syntheses of the masters of the Renaissance. The example of Michelangelo's Piazza di Campidoglio (Fig. 70), where the onlooker has to move past the central statue in order to reach the beginning of the steps towards the main building and thus gain a changing picture of the square, is a very characteristic one. But this principle is also true of real architectural synthesis in every great age of architecture, whether Japanese, Chinese, Mogul or any other great architecture created by man.

This notion of time is perhaps more important in classical Greek architecture than in any of the syntheses I have ever seen, for there it is expressed, not only in motion but also even symbolically, in the unfinished building. There are several elements in the Acropolis of Athens which prove that the architect deliberately left some parts of his building incomplete in order to give visual, material expression to his conception of time as the fourth element of the synthesis. Such is the case with the unfinished Erechtheum, which conveys the impression of the pending completion of the whole synthesis (Fig. 71). Even

Figs. 67 and 68.   The Acropolis of Athens. An example of a perfect architectural synthesis based not on principles devised on the drafting board but on the movement of man walking on the rock

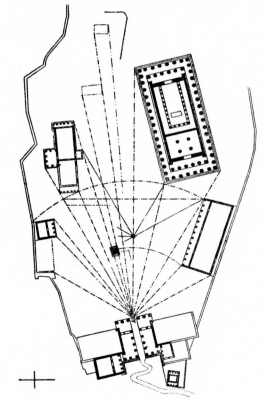

more characteristic is the message of time conveyed by the incomplete
cutting of the marble blocks used in several ancient buildings. On the
Acropolis of Athens this is especially apparent in the walls of the
Propylaea, where the marble blocks have never been completely cut—
although the Acropolis and all its buildings remained in full use for
many centuries after their construction had been completed (Fig. 72).

We can now understand that the notion of time is an indispensable dimension of any architectural synthesis, and for the following
reasons:

(a) A normal architectural synthesis is never completed. It is as
    alive as the people themselves, and it changes with time (Fig.
    73). In the exceptional cases where such a synthesis is finished,

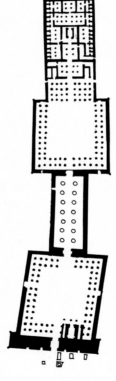

Fig. 69.   The Temple of Ammon in Luxor. The axis of movement changes in
order to express the change by motion

Fig. 70. Michelangelo's Piazza di Campidoglio. In moving past the central statue to
the steps of the main building, the onlooker gains a changing picture of the square

Fig. 71. The unfinished Erechtheum on the Acropolis of Athens conveys the
impression of the pending completion and brings the time factor into the synthesis

and this is the case in a few monumental groups of buildings only (Ancient Greece, Japan, etc.), then the notion of time is conveyed indirectly.

(b) In any case time is required for an architectural experience, since, with the abstraction of time, architecture becomes painting or sculpture.

Time was always the fourth dimension of architecture. It is characteristic, however, that although the first of the above reasons has become even more important because of the acceleration of the

Fig. 72. The unfinished walls of the Propylaea on the Acropolis of Athens convey in structure detail the same message of time dimension

rate of change, architectural experience and expression have become more and more static in our day. This is due in the main to false conceptions of academism and monumentality in every architectural synthesis and to the stagnation of creative forces.

The task ahead of us now is to express the dimension of time more and more in our architecture, simply because it has become more important than ever before.

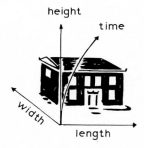

Fig. 73.   A normal architectural synthesis is as alive as
people: it changes with time

6   return to a universal architecture

NOW THAT we have examined our new problems, as well as the new solutions we have evolved to meet them, we can ask ourselves what road we should take. An old Greek saying has it that, 'The gods know of things that shall happen, and men of those things now coming to pass, but wise men of those that are just coming along.'

We ordinary men do not know the future, but we can at least try to get wiser and foresee tomorrow. We can begin to peer into the darkness, to avoid moving erratically or in different directions at once, and so set the single course that is one day to lead us to our ultimate goal. Even if the end of the road is not yet in sight, still we have to start and we can see its beginning.

A certain number of sound and definite principles emerged from our analysis of problems and solutions. One of the most important of these is that 'visiting time' is over so far as architecture is concerned. We must look on architectural creations as objects not merely to be visited but to be lived in. Not only our houses and buildings but also our squares and roads, indeed the whole space surrounding us must be moulded architecturally. Architecture must not be looked upon as one of the sights of the city, as a monument of the past or even of the present. In the golden days of well-balanced architectural styles, a whole city, such as the city of Athens, had a single overall character and its monumental places were simply the highest expression of a common architecture. This is no longer true today, and our present state of affairs must not be allowed to continue.

Speaking of the future of architecture, we must remember the

143

great forces of inertia, habit, vested interest, the impact of our surroundings, conformity, etc., all of which keep us bound to the past.
It is quite natural, therefore, to expect that the ideas accepted today
may come to reality and have an important impact on our architectural habitat in a generation or two, and that ideas to be developed in our generation may make their impact in a century. In this
respect the architecture of the future, unlike industry or art, is proceeding at a comparatively slow pace.

We can now conclude that it is our duty to find the beginning of
our road into the future and to make sure that humanity will follow
it. It is only in this way that we will recognize the real magnitude of
our obligations as pace-makers and thus proceed sooner towards the
realization of our goals. We have to move quickly and decisively and
in a way which will not be threatened by the forces of reaction but
will in fact be so planned as to counteract them and lead us ahead.

A TOTAL ARCHITECTURE

We must clarify our thinking and try to work towards a total architecture. This means a change in the scale of creation. We can no
longer limit ourselves to single buildings, and our idea and ambition
should no longer be to create some monuments through which we
shall influence their surroundings. We should rather work to create
a total architecture inside which we shall re-create our whole living-
space architecturally.

In the past, until the new forces created confusion in our minds,
architecture was always total in every settlement. Then, architecture
was broken into pieces and limited to a few islands of the past and
examples of the future. We have to return to the earlier phase, that of
total architecture, the only one which is natural and consistent.

After all, this is not such a difficult thing to do. On the contrary,
to be consistent in our creation is the only natural solution. Our
new findings have convinced us that not only the single house or
building, not only the square or road, the sector or the town, but a
whole region can follow certain rules of synthesis, rules which we
later find to be the same as those in nature. I have already mentioned
the case of the formation of broader ekistic spaces which are similar
to the calicospheriles or concretions of calcium carbonate (see Fig. 32,

page 98) and I could add that the details of a typical regional plan designed by us reminded Professor Hassan Fathy of Egypt of the structure of a dragonfly's wing (Fig. 74).

In normal periods of evolution architecture was always total. We can and must return to a total architecture whose geographic extent is going to be even larger than in the past as settlements grow from the small city towards the metropolis and the megalopolis, and tend towards the ecumenopolis or universal city which covers whole regions and spreads its complex network all over the earth. For the first time in the history of humanity we can look forward to such an architectural framework and such a new task

A REAL ARCHITECTURE

By expanding enormously and conquering space, architecture will no longer be limited to a few buildings as such, but will become a real architecture, inspired neither by painting nor by sculpture; it will utilize these arts, but will not copy them. Painting, being two-dimensional, cannot become architecture by creating architectural depth; and sculpture, in its turn, is equally unable to become architecture but must necessarily remain static in three dimensions (mobiles are an elementary move of sculpture towards the conquest of the fourth dimension); so in the same way architecture must fulfil itself and be a four-dimensional complex serving the actual needs of the people in a dynamic, not a static, synthesis.

In this way architecture will again use all its elements. It will need all its dimensions, the basic, traditional three: height, length and depth, together with the fourth dimension of time which, although as old as the other three, is gaining a much greater importance in our era. It will utilize time by drawing people into, and allowing people to move about in, its creations.

But we must be sure that we understand the notion of time in the context of the architecture to come. In the past the notion of time was related to a slow growth and to the movement of the pedestrian. Now it is related to a quick growth and to the speed of pedestrian, car, aircraft and rocket. Because of this growth architecture can no longer be based on an introvert synthesis, but must be conceived in a manner allowing for continuous expansion.

K

Fig. 74.   The inner structure of the regional plan for Greater Mussayib
in Iraq (above) is similar to a dragonfly's wing (Doxiadis Associates)

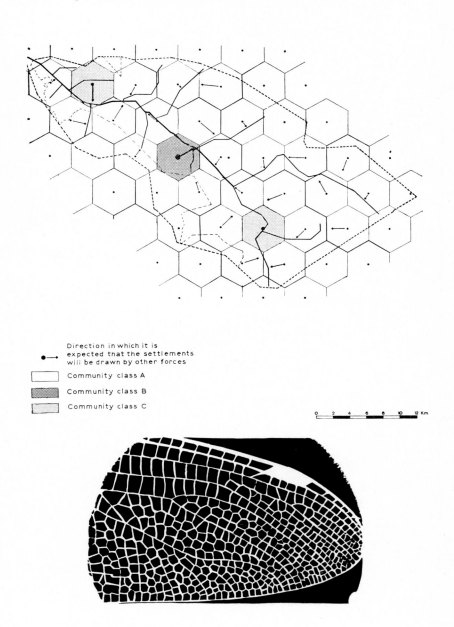

Direction in which it is
expected that the settlements
will be drawn by other forces

Community class A

Community class B

Community class C

Moreover, architecture must be designed to different scales, each of which will require a different set of architectural elements. If we are dealing with a small square meant for pedestrians we have to make sure that all the details, from the size of the pavement-slabs to the very signs on buildings, are on the human scale. If we are dealing with a highway or cloverleaf crossing, however, we will need larger spaces, larger divisions of the concrete surface, much larger signs (if any) and a different handling of the surfaces of all buildings.

Architecture will have to use all the elements it can find, including colour, for colour can come back into our synthesis too. Vincent van Gogh once wrote that the painter of the future would be a colourist as he never was before. This will also be true of architecture which, evolving on a major scale, will need more and more colour in all its expressions. Factors such as prefabrication lead easily to uniformity, and the weaknesses of it can frequently be avoided by proper handling of colour. On the other hand, a factor such as speed makes decoration in the older sense completely superfluous, so that the use of intense colouring for large surfaces becomes much more important than ever before.

By revising our attitude to every single aspect of the architectural synthesis we can have hopes of our architecture again becoming a true expression of our needs and desires. If it does this it will have once more become real architecture.

AN ETERNAL ARCHITECTURE

The question now arises of whether architecture should be traditional, contemporary or an architecture of the future. The answer is simple: architecture should always be contemporary. There is no reason why we should want to imitate the past, nor to build houses only for our grandchildren. We do, however, have the obligation and the right to build for ourselves, and to create an architecture which will not only be contemporary but remain contemporary for as long as possible. This means, first, that we must avoid any tendency to aim at fashion, and limit ourselves to the essentials. To achieve this we shall have to think about construction as well as needs. Moreover, we shall have to build our architecture, not design it. In so doing we shall discover that the more we purge our forms of every inherited element, the more we shall be returning to certain basic traditional forms. It is here that we find the link between tradition and evolution. In an inscription found in the Palace of Priam at Troy we read:

> Yoked to the past, the future takes on a
> body and the word becomes substance.

The more we try to clarify our ideas and reach the most basic and essential forms, the more we find ourselves reaching back towards tradition. I have myself discovered this in many instances. For example, when I tried to purge the architecture of my own flat of everything that was inherited or inspired from outside, so as to make it as rational a dwelling-place as possible, I found myself back at the forms which are the old traditional forms that created the classical Greek style and the Byzantine style, and which can still be seen in Greek villages and monasteries: the interplay of lighter and darker surfaces, together with the rhythmical formation of the lighted ones (Fig. 75).

One thing I have added, and that is what I call the double-skin; the 'canopy' which can be moved up or down, thus guaranteeing to the real skin or external surface of the house all the coolness it requires during the hot season (Figs. 76, 77).

Working in this way we gradually realize that we must put aside fashion or any attempt to copy the trends of either modernism or any other style. We also realize that we must not turn architecture into exhibitionism or formalism but must create something which, although contemporary, will yet be fully adjusted to all our needs, and so remain as eternal as the ancient or perhaps as eternal as the future architecture.

AN URBAN ARCHITECTURE

In thinking of the architecture of our era we have to remember that it tends to be more and more urban as time passes. The term urban architecture, however, can have a variety of meanings. Specifically, it can be thought of as:

(a) A geographic term, as distinct from rustic, open-space architecture.

Fig. 75. Block of flats in Athens: the search for contemporary solutions leads to age-old patterns (C. A. Doxiadis's home)

(b) A cultural term, as distinct from rural, small-town architecture, which is to be identified more with handicrafts than mass production.

(c) A social term, as the architecture of a democratic urban society, as distinct from a feudal or aristocratic society.

Fig. 76.   The double-skin elevation: a natural air-cooling system based on
canopies which have been turned into architectural elements

   (d) An economic term, as distinct from an architecture of special
   buildings only, where economy is not of primary importance.

   To demonstrate the importance of this principle of an urban
architecture it seems necessary to refer to a problem where there is a
great danger of misconception and confusion today because of the
lack of understanding of the urban nature of our architecture. It is
the problem caused by the discovery of new techniques for shell
construction and the attempts to create a spherical or a shell-like
house, where a certain amount of unnecessary confusion has been
created.
   First, cylindrical or spherical houses do not serve man as interiors,
since he lives and moves in space in certain straight lines and not in

Fig. 77. This space is of a different quality. It protects the house from heat and light and allows its adjustment to seasons and hours of the day, without blocking the view

circles; then, almost all elements within a house, such as beds, cupboards, armchairs, sofas, etc., are oblong, and it seems impossible to create an economically feasible synthesis of oblong elements within a circle or an ellipse.

Secondly, we cannot repeat a spherical unit in height. Multi-storey buildings are necessarily based on the synthesis of the vertical and the horizontal, and it is illogical to assume that our needs are going to be covered by rectilinear multi-storey and spherical one-storey buildings.

Thirdly, a spherical house creates many problems for itself, such as that of the flow and drain of water on its roof, lighting, etc.

To these reasons we can add the important fact that humanity has, in its development, passed through the phase of spherical and ellipti-cal houses and gradually come to the rectilinear ones. We cannot turn back the pages of history. We can continue the evolution of architectural species, but not reverse it (Figs. 78, 79).

The fact that shells offer easier construction in several cases should not mislead us into believing that these are the forms which are to survive. The dome was a better type of construction, even in the period of brick construction, but we have not used it universally, nor thought that it could be used in such a way as to turn us from rectangles to circles. Designers of spherical or cylindrical houses justify their creation by terming them economically feasible. It is true, of course, that they do achieve the economy of the shell cover-ing the house, but that is not the real economy at which we must aim. Our problem is not to create a shell for a single family alone, but to create one for many families in an urban settlement. Our aim is not economy in the construction of single units, because this makes no contribution to the general solution. What we must seek is the economy of a total synthesis; that is, the economy of a single form which may be repeated indefinitely. Single houses can be neither cylindrical nor spherical, nor yet covered by shells in non-rectangular shapes, for the simple reason that such shapes cannot be inter-connected to yield an overall synthesis (Fig. 80).

If we try to make a synthesis of such houses we shall realize that we are creating what is in effect a negative space between them. We must not look at space in this negative way, unless indeed we intend completely to abandon the idea of bringing houses together and creating an urban environment, and want merely to distribute them in a wilderness where every house will stand in physical, and indirectly in social, isolation. Thus any synthesis of spherical or cylindrical houses seems impossible, uneconomic and definitely non-urban.

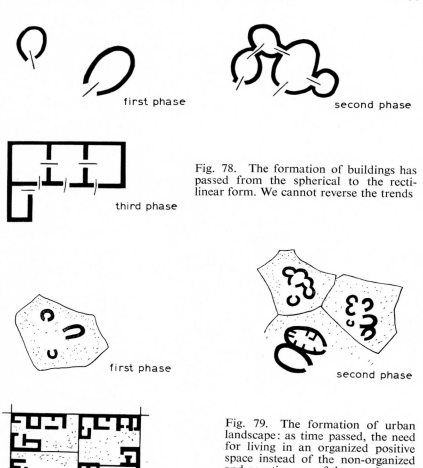

first phase

second phase

Fig. 78. The formation of buildings has passed from the spherical to the recti-linear form. We cannot reverse the trends

third phase

first phase

second phase

Fig. 79. The formation of urban landscape: as time passed, the need for living in an organized positive space instead of the non-organized and negative one of the past became third phase imperative. Natural evolution cannot be halted

We can easily demonstrate, therefore, that the only possible synthesis is one of the vertical and the horizontal, and there is no doubt whatever that it is the building based on vertical and horizontal elements which is going to survive in the future. On the other hand, however, while we may be sure that the spherical house is an impossibility, the shell does seem a reasonable solution for some special types of buildings which are not to be repeated indefinitely either horizontally or in height.

We can thus foresee that the future synthesis will be a synthesis of an urban landscape which is not to be based on shells; furthermore, we cannot expect a revival of the process which led to the Byzantine or the Gothic styles unless the trends are reversed and humanity turns again to an era of religion and great symbols. What we shall look forward to is the construction of large buildings and the greatest parts of our cities on the basis of the repetition of the horizontal and the vertical.

We can expect, to be sure, that our future synthesis will demand the use of both horizontal-vertical lines and shells. The basic element of our synthesis for a long time will be the low house repeated over large areas, together with the multi-storey building in conjunction with domes and shells for exceptional buildings (Fig. 81).

It is not the first time in our history that this has happened, for the Ancient Greeks, facing the same dilemma, were forced to the same

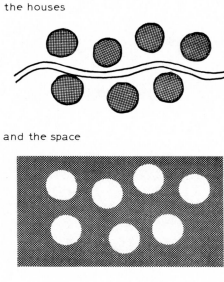

Fig. 80. Circular houses cannot become parts of an urban synthesis. They lead us back towards primitiveness

conclusion; that is, that they could indeed use the round element in their synthesis, but only for special purposes (Fig. 82).

In every aspect of the architecture which we must develop we can recognize the ever-increasing influence of the urban contemporary element. If we ask ourselves what is the most characteristic influence of this prevailing urban element we will find that it is the proper density of habitation. This is so because it is only through proper habitation density that we achieve:

(a) human scale in practical and aesthetic terms
(b) economy in the utilization of space
(c) best possible micro-climate
(d) economy in function and maintenance.

By achieving the proper density we have answered the most important demand of urban architecture—to create a proper space to live in.

A HUMAN ARCHITECTURE

Since we stated as a principle that our architecture is meant to serve man and not the machine, or any special category of men such as kings, lords or priests, it is obvious that architecture must also be human. This can be achieved principally by building in our urban space, whether public or private, on the human scale. Without proper scale there is no human architecture, but scale alone is not enough. Architecture should be human in all its aspects.

There is an age-old need, for example, to protect some sides of our buildings from the sun, either throughout the year or at least during the summer. At the beginning and for tens of centuries the natural solution was to build a verandah, which occasionally even took the form of a monumental 'stoa'. In some countries the same protection was achieved for certain parts of the buildings by means of a perforated screen.

In our generation, however, we have witnessed attempts to solve the same old problem through the use of horizontal or vertical sun-breakers, which also unfortunately acted as dust-collectors and light-reflectors. In this way man was enclosed within his building, and

Fig. 81.   The elements of a logical urban synthesis will be the
        rectilinear buildings with some shells between them

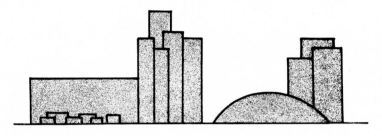

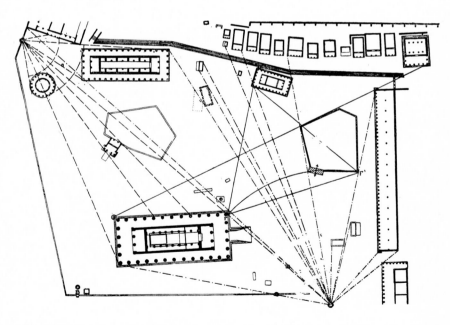

Fig. 82.   The Altis of Olympia: an age-old example of a synthesis of many
        rectilinear buildings with only a single circular one

very often not even allowed an unobstructed view of the outside world; his home was thus turned into a prison. There have even been attempts to use perforated screens which covered whole buildings like a skin, with the overall result that man was condemned to live or work inside an eternal prison. Such solutions are indeed inhuman and artificial (Fig. 83), and do not lead to proper human architecture. But, if properly employed, they can be turned into human solutions. It is not necessary for sun-breakers to be at the eye-level of the people sitting or standing inside a building. Moreover, the surfaces of the sun-breakers can be handled so as to avoid completely the reflection of light or the collection of dust, as has been demonstrated in types of buildings designed for Islamabad, the new capital of Pakistan (Fig. 84). Every architectural element should be handled in a way that will create a human architecture (Fig. 85).

TOWARDS SIMILAR SOLUTIONS

If we follow the trends towards a total urban architecture which is to be real and lasting we will discover that we are gradually led towards a similarity of solutions for different parts of the world as well as for different kinds of buildings. Personally, after having worked in some fifteen different countries and having tried to give expression to my ideas in as local a manner as possible, I must confess that I have very often been led to similar solutions regardless of the country I was in. Everywhere I went I tried to develop the local styles, explaining that architecture must not be imposed but should grow like a young tree in the local soil and sun. I tried to emphasize that architecture must grow over the generations from the seed that we place in the earth into the sturdy and stately tree we want it to become.

This is still my belief, but I often found that my plants persisted in showing many similarities, despite my effort to plant a different seed at each place. There were many forces compelling me to adopt similar solutions, so that although I started every time with the ardent desire to be influenced only by the locality—and was so influenced— still I could not forget certain major factors which are bound to influence architectural creation in the future. Thus quite often, although certainly not always, I found myself offering parallel solutions to different problems in places as far apart as Pakistan and

Fig. 83.   Protection of buildings from the rays of the sun
through the use of different systems

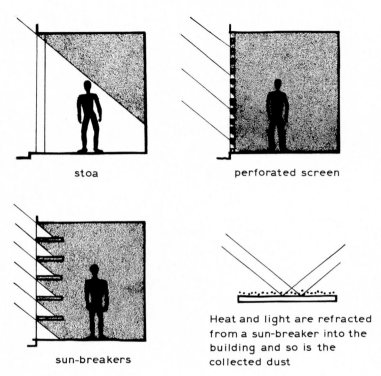

Greece, the U.S.A., the Middle East or Africa. These solutions might
look different to the inexperienced eye because they varied in some
aspects, but they were in fact substantially one and the same solution
at bottom. This suggests that solutions in our age are inevitably
similar, even though they may be expressed differently; for certainly
a house in the Middle East may and does look completely different
from a house in America or Africa.

When I was confronted by this situation I had to answer an important question. I said to myself: 'I frequently tend to adopt similar
solutions. Should I consciously try to be different?' I came to the
conclusion that I had no right to be different where the conditions
themselves compelled me to remain the same. We should not be
afraid to express ourselves in the same way and repeat something that

Fig. 84. Protection of buildings in Islamabad (Doxiadis Associates). The sun-breakers don't turn the building into a prison and the handling of their surface completely eliminates their deficiencies. This is a completed solution

room with sun-breakers

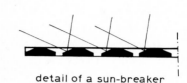

detail of a sun-breaker

is good. After all, the doctor is not afraid to prescribe a medicine simply because it has been used before. We are not afraid to build walls using identical bricks, nor do we keep to the old polygonic system of the walls of Delphi. We can equally easily build beautiful or ugly walls with the very same bricks—the important thing is the kind of bricks we use and how we use them.

In this way, however, we are moving towards uniformity in several aspects of our work, and one might ask anxiously whether such a uniformity of solutions might not lead to a uniformity of houses and therefore of appearances too. This is definitely not inevitable. We are obliged to be true to ourselves and to build in the best possible way every time, without trying to be traditional or academic, but also without trying to be 'modern' or trying to discover something new in every case.

Let us turn our minds back to earlier periods of history when people were producing on the same patterns. Let us take Ancient Greece first. Classical Greece had one style for several centuries, but we never speak of a uniformity of appearance there, for we never feel one: we never protest about the similar appearance of all Greek columns. The Doric as well as the other styles certainly had its canons yet every temple was a piece of art in its own right. Although the simple houses had approximately the same plan throughout Greece, still they were not uniform.

Fig. 85. Human architecture in Islamabad (Doxiadis Associates). Preliminary design for the administrative blocks. The buildings remain cool and clean and people control the space

This is also true in Egyptian art. The Egyptian craftsmen were working on the basis of canons imposed by the priestly caste; nevertheless, they did not produce a standardized art. Do we not find any piece of Egyptian painting or sculpture an equally interesting object of art?

It was the same in Byzantine times, when the monks painted according to the very strict canons of the age and of their religion. Yet is not every piece of true Byzantine art a different masterpiece?

We should not be afraid of having a similarity of solutions, a similarity of rhythms, underlying our syntheses. We are now tending to standardization, which leads to the rhythmical repetition of an identical pattern of construction. We need not avoid that just because it is rational, nor need we avoid building whole cities on the basis of one and the same modulus; a modulus which is to underlie the town plan, the layout plan, the plan of the plot and the formation of the building itself. Do we not write our music on certain scales? It is not necessarily either good or bad music just because of that. Whether it is good or bad depends entirely on the synthesis we achieve.

We should not avoid certain patterns of construction, for in certain cases we are bound to follow a logical pattern of rhythmical repetition. Such a repetition is necessary for the rational formation of many parts of such buildings as schools, hotels, hospitals and private houses. It is also necessary for the improvement and standardization of construction, as well as for prefabrication. Finally, it is also necessary, although not indispensable, from an aesthetic point of view.

Where is the repetition of the classical Greek temple, the Italian palazzo, the halls in the Red Fort of Delhi or the dome of the Sistine Chapel, leading us? Why did Michelangelo keep to a rhythmical repetition when he could have given his subject another solution and developed it in a much more independent way?

Whenever I think of this I am reminded of the advice which a great Greek poet, Kostes Palamas, gave to the craftsman:

> Hand bound, imagination bound,
> The artisan carving the image of God
> To the priests' dictates,
> Swaddling it in the traditional way,
> Still finds some place to lay
> His own heart's love for it, the image,
> So that making your obeisance
> You yearn towards it that way, oh people,
> That way worshipping before it, oh people.

The fact that we are led towards similar solutions should not frighten us but should rather challenge us to create an architecture with its own character.

TOWARDS CONSISTENT EXPRESSION

We have reached a point at which we are challenged to create an architecture with a character, or perhaps we should say a style, of its own. Now we must consider the phase of evolution through which our architecture is passing, the phase of evolution usually related to the creation of styles.

In ancient times a style was created by a gradual process of selection and evolution from the best types of houses and buildings being created in a certain area, within the framework of the developing tastes of that area. It was a process that took centuries, but since it was carried out at the level of the whole society it also led to forms acceptable by the whole society.

This process no longer occurs and we have already seen that there is at present a large gap between the need for architecture and our actual architectural achievement (see Fig. 7, page 46), a gap which we are trying to fill. Our architecture, however, is no longer in the hands of the master builders, who represented the normal, slow evolution, but in those of architects who have had to be trained in schools, and our architectural questions have therefore over the last few generations been decided among the people designing and ordering monumental buildings. During this latter period there has been no need for co-ordination with the people, for this movement began with a small class who wanted to create styles. It began at the level of the intellectuals and certain representatives of the leading classes of the Western world who at different times wanted to see the Ancient Greek or the Egyptian or any of a variety of other styles revived or re-created as the *art nouveau* or modern architecture of their countries. But the situation has changed, and this dictatorship of a small group of intellectuals over the field of architecture is now beginning to lose its importance (Fig. 86).

The situation is different today because the architect must now build for the masses, creating architecture for everybody and not for a certain leading class alone. It follows that he has to build much

Fig. 86. The architect's activity throughout the world

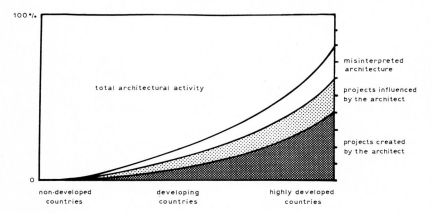

greater numbers of houses and buildings, and it is in this way that we are gradually returning to the age of natural styles. We cannot now impose upon everyone an artificial style—even a good one—which has been created at the top of the cone, but must instead find some way of serving all our needs in a way acceptable to all the people. This can be achieved not by lowering our standards but by making them correspond to the actual needs and possibilities of the people. Then some day monumental architecture may gradually reappear, of itself, at the top of the cone. This will be the first time that, while guiding our total efforts by the lights of a leading class of architects, we shall in fact be working from the base of the cone upwards—the first time that architects will be responsible for consciously creating a style without having first conceived it in a vacuum.

True styles grew by themselves in the past, and were as natural a product of their area as the trees and vegetation. Now we have the difficult task of trying to let a new architecture grow, but we have to do it consciously. What was simply allowed to happen in the past must now be consciously created.

We have defined how we want our architecture to be created and how we want it to grow. We have set ourselves a rule which we cannot ignore whenever we are talking about architecture in the broadest sense of the word; from the creation of styles to the creation of houses, buildings, specific plans, cities and so forth. That is why many of the solutions now being proposed for the city of the future and the

architecture of the future are unacceptable: they simply do not constitute a normal evolution from our own times.

We must not forget that while progress appears at the top of the
cone of creation, it can spread over large areas and influence our total
activity only if it is developed in a normal way from the base of that
same cone. For example, progress may lead us to the idea of an aluminium spherical house, but if this is not the evolution of the total of
our methods of construction, and most people continue to build
with brick and stone, then we cannot speak of having a continuous
process moving towards the top of the cone, but only of an experi-
ment in an idiom suited to another environment or another age. That
is why we must seek developing solutions in every case, solutions
which will have in them the elements of evolution.

We must try to find the continuity which relates the simplest to the
most highly developed solutions, because only thus can we build a
whole system leading to a new architecture which will also be a new
style. Every important solution in the past which did not represent
a normal development has remained with us merely as an isolated
example, with no influence whatever on the overall evolution.

It is clear, then, that it is still too early to speak of the creation of
styles. What we must do is to create an architecture with character.
To achieve this, however, we need a continuity in all our efforts, and
this is possible only through a consistent expression at all levels of
the cone of architectural creation and for all sizes of architectural
space.

Consistency we must have, and we have first to define the area
within which we will look for such consistency. This is directly related
to the number of people influencing architectural creation, which in
turn depends on the progress of communications of all kinds and the
area over which these communications are possible.

Architectural creation, as we have already seen, began in the past
at the local level, where it was under the influence of one man. Under
the impact of civilization and expanding internal communications,
more and more people entered the scene and made their contribution.
In so doing, they turned architecture from an unco-ordinated personal
expression into a local expression, having a character which could
under favourable conditions become a local style. As time passed,
architecture spread to a broader regional and then an international

Fig. 87.   Architectural creation in relation to time, space and number of
people contributing to it

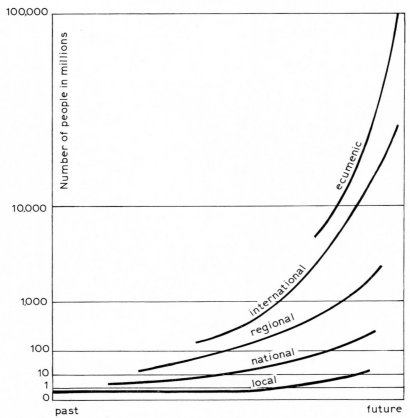

level. Finally, in our era, it is beginning to become ecumenic or universal, with ever more people contributing to its creation and ever more difficulties to hinder its consistent expression (Fig. 87).

BACK TO AN ECUMENIC ARCHITECTURE

Present trends prove beyond doubt that we are in fact moving towards an ecumenic architecture. This will first become consistent within itself; it will then acquire its own ecumenic character, and may at length develop into a universal style. We are gradually moving not only towards similar solutions but towards solutions which are themselves basic to humanity and not bound to a particular locality. One fundamental reason for this is the socialization of architecture. So long as architecture was limited to the desires and styles of a ruling class, whether its proffered lead was intellectual, administrative or any other kind, architecture was still quite able to express the desires of such a class in its own particular isolated society.

Now that the boundaries between cultures have been broken through, however, and we are being drawn together towards a common culture, architecture must serve the broadest classes of people everywhere. People are basically the same, so we are gradually moving towards an ecumenic expression through trying to create our architecture in the simplest possible way, in order to be able to serve everybody.

In coming into closer contact, people can gradually find the best solutions in conception and detail, not through a copying of forms but through a gradual selection by the many.

This selection operates in all directions, as for example where the West in many respects now follows the style of the Mogul screens (Fig. 88) created centuries ago, or the Japanese methods of pre-fabricating panels of construction, or even the Japanese conception of the garden. It is through such principles of gradual selection that we are moving towards universal solutions.

These examples remind us that the influences at work no longer always necessarily radiate outwards towards the other countries from the central framework embracing the Western universities. We must remember that a contracting world has drawn people together, so that while the less-developed countries benefit by the experience gained in the more highly developed ones, the latter gain at the same time from their less-experienced counterparts. People are now becoming aware of solutions which are considered very modern in the Western world, but which are already very old in the East, and several Western architects have already begun to study diligently the lessons to be learned from other countries. One of them, Dr. Ezra D. Ehrenkrantz, has even appealed for technical assistance to over-developed countries.

For example, as long as the colonizing powers, whether Greek, Roman or British, were imposing a particular style on other countries, there was no real relationship between that style and the people. Now

Fig. 88. An age-old solution given monumental expression by the great Moguls
is now being rediscovered by the world

there is no longer any question of imposing styles of any kind on any-body, for people are everywhere selecting for themselves. We are thus gradually absorbing into our thinking solutions which are age-old; we are reclassifying and re-evaluating everything.

The idea of the creation of an ecumenic architecture poses yet another basic question. Did man ever possess an ecumenic style in the past? I think we must assert that he did. He may not have been conscious of it, because it existed at an early stage of his civilization, but it did exist. In fact, it still exists throughout the countryside of many, if not all, countries.

If we examine simple houses in Asia, Africa or in the Mediter-ranean, we shall find that they are indistinguishable even to the expert eye (Figs. 89, 90).

Protracted journeys through many countries have convinced me that at the beginning of every civilization there existed the same elementary style. It was the different types of civilization growing up in different centres that led man towards local expressions in art, these expressions differing from area to area as civilizations developed more and more independently and in isolation from one another. The Egyptians, Greeks, Romans and lately the British certainly attempted to impose their own styles on other people, but as these styles were

Fig. 89.   A house under the Himalayas (Murree Hills, West Pakistan) has many similarities with the Greek houses which led to the formation of the Ancient Greek styles

imposed from the top downwards, as official styles, they never really took root. We are being led back to a style which will be ecumenic because it will be basically human and because the whole of developing civilization is tending to similar patterns.

We must not be misled by the fact that some people, rightly or wrongly, are bound to conceive of alternative solutions; if these cannot spread so as to control the whole cone of human creation it will be impossible for them to take root and influence architecture as a whole.

Architecture cannot be the brainchild of the few. It will have to be, indeed it must again become, the child of humanity as a whole. This is because, irrespective of technological evolution and special solutions for specific cases, we are going to have an architecture which will grow and because the same solutions will be repeatable on a large scale only under certain circumscribing conditions. What are those conditions?

First, they must be acceptable to all people in all countries, a condition it becomes more difficult to fulfil as evolution progresses everywhere, and people become more and more aware of their needs and rights and so are less apt to be influenced by imported solutions. Second, the solutions must also be practical, economical and basically good enough to serve the broadest masses of the people. In this respect, real architectural evolution will in fact depend more on the rate of increase of the income of all the nations in the world than on the ability of a few to conceive highly developed monumental or economic projects.

The top of our cone is going to be sound only if it rests on solid foundations. It seems certain that the new human, ecumenic architecture is going to be formalized at the top of the human cone, but it will prove successful only if the ideas coming from the top are reflected to the base and then reflected upwards again (Fig. 91).

If this human, ecumenic architecture is to survive and develop into a style it must not be limited to the mental or economic capacity of the few. It must have a broad basis or it will not take root; it will become stagnant, as was the fate of some imported styles. The styles which were able to survive over long periods in particular areas were those that were well and deeply rooted in the soil of their country, as was the case with the styles of Classical Greece, Renaissance Italy

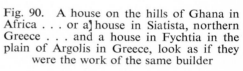

Fig. 90.   A house on the hills of Ghana in
Africa . . . or a house in Siatista, northern
Greece . . . and a house in Fychtia in the
plain of Argolis in Greece, look as if they
were the work of the same builder

or Imperial Japan. With such an ecumenic style we can create an architecture which will be human in both its conception and content while remaining local in its expression.

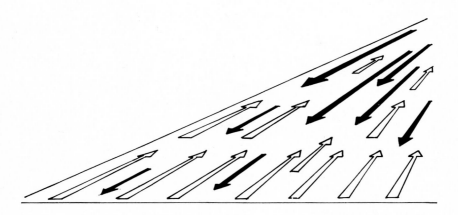

Fig. 91. The proper creation of architecture in our time: natural forces from the base of the cone have to merge with forces from the top down

7   laying the foundations

IT IS not enough to know of the rising tide of problems and the broad trend of the colossal changes that are taking place. The moment has now come for us to define our attitudes and prepare a blueprint for action.

We have seen ourselves, so far, breasting a sea of architectural confusion, bewildered by problems and crises; we have defined the architect's role and responsibility, and have established what meagre influence he in fact has over contemporary movements. Moreover, we have surveyed the new problems and sensed the new solutions that they require. Finally, we have seen that we must move from the traditional to the contemporary, from the local to the universal, and that we are returning to an ecumenic architecture.

What should our attitude be? Should we play the passer-by, or should we be like a historian following trends and tracking down the course of events; should we be passive in our attitude or should we be the pace-makers guiding humanity on the basis of the trends we uncover, but keeping the whole situation well in hand?

There can be no question that we ought to be free not only to study the trends but also to define a policy towards them, to define our role and become the leaders of the evolution to come.

There are many big problems to be faced and we must emphasize again the significance of clarifying how we want to live. We must remember the great importance of this simple word 'we' in its social content, and take decisions which have a deep democratic importance; for we must define the role of the expert as that of the leader of a democratic movement and the interpreter of the people's desires. We must define, too, how we want our habitat to be formed, how we can clarify what people really mean when they say that they want to live in a certain way. Finally, we must define the notion of living—whether it is to be confined within the four walls of a building, or whether it is to be something much broader and much more important.

To face all this, we must now prepare a programme for action, a schedule of work. In this programme we must specify our role in the great problems that we are facing and take a definite stand on all practical issues. Only in this way can we succeed—and, even if we do not, we shall at least have the satisfaction of knowing that we have done our duty towards the great subject in which we are supposed to be the experts.

DEFINITION OF THE SUBJECT

In order to lay the foundations for the architecture of the future and prepare the proper programme of action, we have to start with a definition of our subject which can be generally accepted. We must, that is, find out what architecture is and what it is trying to do.

We must first remind ourselves that architecture is the discipline not of designing houses or buildings, much less of designing monuments, but of building the human habitat. As such it consists of a science, a technique and an art.

It order to create a better architecture—that is, a better habitat—we have to assist in the creation of a better way of living. Although this is not the task of the architect alone, the architect can certainly play a very important role in several aspects of this great problem.

How great this problem is can be understood if we think of how little attention we pay today to the notion of living, as against the notion of moving, in several industrialized countries. The most characteristic example of this new trend is the great importance attached by many people to their car, in contrast to their relative indifference towards their house. The new trends, the new problems, which arise in this field can be seen also in the increasing number and importance of caravan camps, of people living in trailer homes; these are the first signs of a new drift, the drift to nomadism in our society.

Architecture has to contribute to the solution of these problems and especially to the concept of a proper way of living which will lead to the proper type of human habitat.

In order to achieve these ends architecture has to be seen as a discipline meant to serve everyone, to house everyone, to create the proper habitat for every citizen of the world. Much more, it has to be seen as a service provided for the people of the world, and not as an art or a mental exercise in the abstract. Furthermore, we must be aware that we cannot limit architecture to the creation, much less to the design, of buildings to be put together on a layout which has nothing to do with their conception and their creation.

For this purpose we have to reunite the conception and creation of the layout with the conception and creation of the buildings. To do this, we have to divide the human habitat not into special aspects of the same physical unit, but into units of different sizes. This means specifically that we cannot afford to leave the layout as the exclusive domain of a certain speciality—let us say town planning—and the buildings to another, say architecture. This is like letting one architect design the plan and another the elevation of a building. We have to entrust the same man or group of men with the creation of a total unit.

Such a unit can no longer be the single building. It has to be a community of a minor class, a community within which the architect will have full responsibility for the conception and the creation of the proper human habitat. It seems to me that such a unit should be one which is controlled by the human scale, and such is only the human community, within which man alone is the controlling factor.

ARCHITECTURE AND EKISTICS

In defining architecture as the discipline of building the human habitat, we especially noted two points: that the architect has to contribute to the conception of the human habitat, and also that he has to limit himself to minor units of that habitat up to a certain size. Both these points are necessary in order to define the real limitations of our discipline, for architecture cannot answer all problems of the human habitat.

In more specific terms, this means that architecture has to find a physical solution to the problem of the human habitat, conceiving this in collaboration with a number of other disciplines included within the broader framework of ekistics, the total science of human settlements. Architecture gives the final physical answer for minor units of the human habitat up to the human community. In this respect, architecture has to be seen as a part of ekistics, no longer as regards the differentiation between the layout of a city and the creation of buildings in it, but rather as regards the differentiation between conceiving the whole human habitat (ekistics) and giving expression to the smallest reasonable units of it (architecture). In this spirit a number of units of architecture taken together form a city or an urban area; but these areas are in the domain of urbanism where the role of architecture is clearly an auxiliary one.

If we move from the urban area to the conception and creation of the region where we have a balance of urban and rural development, then the role of architecture becomes even smaller, and it is regionalism which takes on the overall responsibility.

In this way we have defined architecture as a part of ekistics, having to deal with a series of units in the following way:

(a) with rooms (non-subdivided, built-up spaces designed and built by the architect with or without the contribution of the interior decorator). These units do not grow, but are static in size;

(b) single houses or buildings, which are created by the architect but can be conceived as growing, expandable and changing units;

(c) the human community, which is designed and created by the architect and does not grow;

(d) the cities, growing organisms created by the urbanists, but with only a minor degree of collaboration from the architect; and

(e) the regions, which do not grow and within which architecture plays an even more minor role than in cities.

The order we have taken brings out the fact that the physical units with which the architect deals form an alternating series—one not growing, one growing, one not growing, one growing, one not growing—as rooms, buildings, human communities, dynamic cities and regions succeed one another.

Architecture in space plays a great role in minor units and a diminishing one as the units grow large. The development of architecture in the future will regulate the degree of its inter-relation and interdependence with other disciplines. The influence of architecture should not be missing even from the synthesis of the largest unit, that is from ecumenopolis; but before it can play this role architecture has to mature in its role and responsibilities (Fig. 92).

FROM MASONS TO MASTER MASONS

The architects of the past started as masons and, through proper evolution, were turned into master masons. Now, these master masons, the architects of the present, will have to occupy themselves with architecture in a scientific manner.

But if we look around to see how far we can carry out our responsibilities, which are indeed enormous, we have to note these facts:

(a) we are very few, certainly not more than 5 per cent of the number required with present standards even for just the design of buildings;

(b) we are confined to the role of the designer of buildings and not permitted the role of master builder; and

(c) we are very badly equipped to play our real role in developing the proper human habitat.

To be really honest with ourselves, we must confess that most of us are suffering from the dangerous disease of megalomania. Most of us may some day find ourselves in the position of a First World War colonel who addressed his troops to gear them for a great attack; much to his surprise, when the time of actual battle came, none of his troops followed him but stood there shouting, 'Bravo, Colonel.' There is great danger that the architect of the present will not be followed by his natural army of masons and builders who in actual practice are producing the human habitat. This is mainly due to the fact that, instead of growing from mason to master builder as in the past, the

Fig. 92.   Total ekistic activity

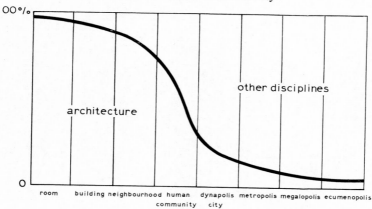

architect is now supposed to start at the top of the cone and go down to the very roots—a task which he seldom accomplishes.

In order to avoid the danger of finding ourselves outside architectural creation we have to rediscover our proper role. The architect must identify himself once more with the builder contractor: he must enter the building industry in all its phases, play his role in the production of the building materials and participate in the construction of buildings. He should not be afraid to return to his age-old role of being the real builder of architecture. But in addition he has to understand that he must also be a manager, a planner, an administrator, a scientist and an artist. As such, he has to enter not only industry and production but also government centres of research and education; in short, every place where real architecture is born.

The question arises now as to how we can reconcile the fact that we are very few and very badly equipped for our role with the demand for a much greater activity in the production of architectural space. The answer can lie only in the proper organization of architects and their preparation for a new role in the future (Fig. 93).

A new organization of our forces must be based on the redefinition of the subject of architecture and the unit of architectural creation—the human community. In order to serve such a human community in the best possible way, we need one group of developers who will be in charge of it. We cannot allow many people to develop different parts or aspects of it simultaneously, because this will lead

M

Fig. 93.   Architectural organization

What happens now is confusion because many
architects are involved in every project but only
in a small part of it

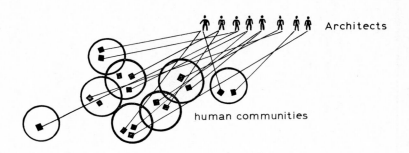

But what we need is organization allowing for
one group of architects to take over every single
human community

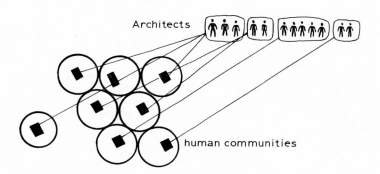

to waste and confusion. This idea naturally takes us to the notion of
having a single group of architects for each architectural unit in each
community. It is only too true that we waste a great deal of precious
time nowadays by allowing too many architects who do not belong
to the same group to be concerned with one architectural unit. This
confusion comes about in two ways:

(a) if the architectural unit is split into too many parts and several architects are in charge of each part, or

(b) if many architectural groups are invited to work on the same architectural unit even if they are co-ordinated.

In this way we are led towards a passive architectural expression, or what we might call architecture by compromise.

In order to be consistent in what we are doing, we have to create architecture by organizing ourselves so as to have:

(a) One physical unit, the human community.

(b) One group of developers per physical unit.

(c) One group of architects participating in the development of the community as a member of the developers' organization.

Whilst this is happening at the local level, architects have also to become members of the teams which decide indirectly on architecture at other levels. They have to become members of the teams of urbanists who are in charge of cities, of the teams of regionalists who decide on the future of regions, of the complete and overall ekistic teams which define the ekistic policies for all human settlements, of the industry which produces the materials and elements of architecture and, finally, of the administration which takes decisions related to architecture.

In order to achieve all this we need far more and better-trained architects, because it is only in this way that we shall achieve any results worthy of the name of architecture and bring an end to the era of confusion.

Furthermore, we need programmes and plans for the training of such architects, who should be looked upon not as a species of meteorites who will dazzle humanity for a brief moment with their new designs, but as the pioneers who, after proper education and painstaking effort, will one day produce for us the better world we seek in architecture.

The discussion of problems concerning the proper role and the proper organization of architects brings to light the question of the size of the teams which are in charge of architectural creation. I purposely do not speak of architectural offices, which are a creation of the present and the recent past, but of architectural teams, in order to include the groups of master masons who were active in the past. If we follow the evolution of these architectural teams we shall see (Fig. 94) that they are of three sizes: small, medium and large.

In the very distant past such teams were very small in size, but as time passed these small teams diminished in number, merging to form teams of medium size. These small teams included the master masons of Ancient Greece and the Middle Ages, the monument-makers. Later on, in the recent past, the number of small teams increased once more as soon as the architects became a product of the universities; but the prospect for the future is that they will again decrease in number and eventually disappear altogether.

The number of teams of medium size is constantly growing and will grow with the progress of civilization until the creation of schools of architectural design brings out architects working by themselves or in very small offices. These medium-sized teams will also tend to disappear in the future.

The large architectural teams, or rather architectural offices, have

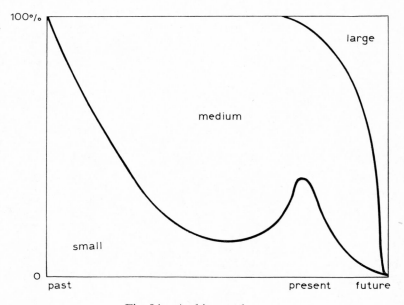

Fig. 94.   Architectural teams

emerged only during the last few generations. They will tend to increase in number until, for the many reasons we have analysed, they gain full control of the situation.

Are these trends good or not? The answer is that whether good or bad they are the outcome of natural forces, of new types of production and new types of organization in our urban life. There is a great danger that in these large offices which will control the situation in the future private initiative and proper development of creative thought may be stamped out, and that the architects themselves may not be mature enough for their new and more difficult task.

It thus becomes one of the most important duties of the architect to be prepared for the creation of the proper type of major architectural teams within which the proper evolution of ideas and creative thought will not merely be safeguarded but also actively encouraged. Until such time it is better to be aware of the danger, and delay the elimination of small and medium-sized offices, even though these may be uneconomical and wasteful from the point of view of productivity and total achievement.

We must be aware that we are inevitably tending towards larger groupings and larger organizations, but we must grow up to the demands of such situations in order to avoid disaster. The more slowly we let the big organizations take over completely, the better it will be for the future of both architects and architecture.

FROM LOCAL TO ECUMENIC

We have already seen that architecture moves from local to ecumenic expressions and that this, being the result of much greater forces which are related to the evolution of our civilization, is an unavoidable trend. We are sure, that is, that the general trends are all leading to an ecumenic architecture; yet we do not know how, where and what kind of ecumenic architecture we are going to have.

To understand the how, the where and the what of this transition from local to ecumenic expressions we must look back for a moment and grasp the process by which local architecture was created in the past, for only in this way can we illuminate the future trends and understand our role.

Local architecture was created in the past by every culture and

Fig. 95.   Architectural evolution in isolated societies

(a) Architectural evolution in isolated societies in thousands of years

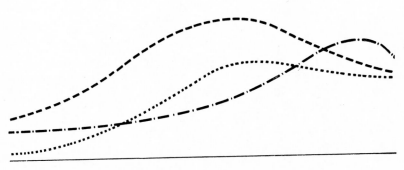

(b) Architectural evolution in isolated societies in centuries

every civilization. Sometimes it was a natural expression of architectural needs; at other times, depending on many factors, it led to an architectural style.

But to understand past evolution better, we have to divide local architectural creation into two categories: that of isolated societies and that of merging societies. Let us take first the creation of architecture in isolated societies. If we plot a graph of this phenomenon in terms of thousands of years, presenting the quality of architectural achievement as its vertical axis and time as its horizontal one, we shall see that every local isolated civilization presents an undulating curve quite unrelated to the other isolated societies (Fig. 95a).

If we look at the same phenomenon on the minor scale of a few centuries, and not of thousands of years, then we shall see the same unco-ordinated evolution of local architectures, the curves for some of which move up while those for others move down (Fig. 95b). In none of these cases is there any similarity between the curves for different local architectures; indeed, when we consider the matter, there is really no reason why there should be any. Similarly, since there is no contact between these isolated civilizations, there is also no imitation of the architectural expressions between societies, although many such societies may start from similar types of architecture.

Now let us take our second category, for evolution is different where societies are no longer isolated, but are merging together. In such cases, regardless of the previous course of architecture, there is a trend towards the same type of evolution from the moment when the societies cease to remain isolated and begin to merge into a broader society covering a broader space (Fig. 96).

If we now try to look at the total architectural activity we shall see that in the distant past (this is not a chronological, but a phase notion) architectural creation was both local and ecumenic. It was local in its expression because of the many local factors which were influencing it. But it was also ecumenic because there was a common denominator of human needs and human expressions not influenced by local civilizations. But with the evolution of local civilizations, architectural expression became more local and gradually lost many

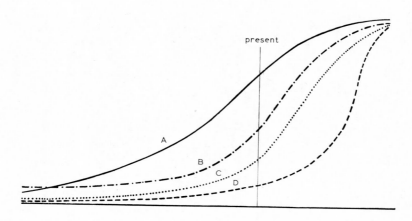

Fig. 96.   Architectural evolution in merging societies: architecture
tends towards similar expressions

of its ecumenic characteristics. This tendency reached a peak before the civilizations of this earth began to merge into one another towards an ecumenic civilization. From that moment on, the trend has definitely been one towards an elimination of all local expressions (Fig. 97).

When are we going to reach this phase of an earth covered by an ecumenic architecture? Evidently, when we are able to have the same type of industry everywhere, the same economic conditions, as well as the same type of prefabrication, the same organization of production and the same type of society. This implies that differences in technological development from area to area will be minimized as a result of an equalization of income. It also means that there will be a dense system of transportation so that all localities can be supplied with prefabricated architectural elements with equal facility.

When speaking in such terms we shall have to be realistic, and accept that this means that, even if we wished, we could not achieve a totally ecumenic architecture before the end of the twenty-first century. In the meantime there will be countries and parts of countries exhibiting definite progress towards an ecumenic architecture.

Such an evolution in some countries will have an impact on the rest which, although not economically or industrially ripe for an ecumenic architecture, will still tend towards one because of the tendency to imitate, if for no other reason. We shall therefore have some hybrid solutions between local and ecumenic which will, however, as ecumenic forces increase and spread, tend to be more and more consistent, more and more honest in their expression.

It now seems that before humanity can reach the phase of an ecumenic architecture it is likely to pass through several phases, during which we shall find our world divided into the following zones of architecture:

(a) zones of ecumenic architecture under development;
(b) zones of local architecture as yet untouched by the ecumenic trends; and
(c) zones of hybrid architecture.

The success of the architectural solution in each case, during this period of transition, will depend on the ability of the architect to:

(a) recognize the phase of evolution through which the locality he serves is passing; and

(b) at the same time respect, as far as possible, the requirements of both ecumenic and local nature, in order to find the best possible balance between them at that particular moment in time.

What is ecumenic architecture going to be? And is it going to be the same everywhere? If we take the view that present trends will continue it certainly seems that way. But this will not be true if, in spite of the unifying forces (tendency to similar incomes, industrialization, prefabrication, organization, etc.), there are local factors, such as climate, sun, light and landscape, which cannot be changed. This means that the orientation of buildings, the architectural synthesis (less dense in the colder climates, more dense in the hotter climates) and the desire for the greatest possible economy for the achievement of a practical project, are going to force us to respect the local requirements more and more.

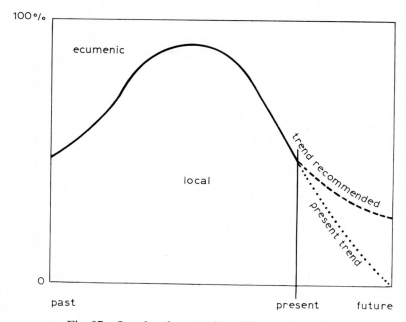

Fig. 97. Local and ecumenic architectural creation

N

This means that our architecture will have the same ecumenic character overall, but that the solutions will vary from locality to locality and thus create a different impression in each.

All these factors lead to the general conclusion that we are tending towards ecumenic architecture. But if we allow trends to continue as at present we shall find ourselves disregarding local forces and moving towards an architecture which will be controlled 100 per cent by ecumenic forces. This would be an unfortunate development, and we have to be careful to preserve as far as possible all those local forces which should have an influence on architecture. Only in this way will we achieve the proper balance between ecumenic and local forces.

FROM TRADITIONAL TO CONTEMPORARY

In contrasting the local with the ecumenic, we are in fact also contrasting the traditional with the contemporary, since traditional architecture is bound to a locality whilst contemporary architecture is mainly influenced by ecumenic trends. We should not be misled into believing, however, that the problem of the local as against the ecumenic is the same as the problem of the traditional as against the contemporary, because, although local expression is very much related to tradition, ecumenic expression is not necessarily contemporary. It is true that future solutions will tend to be ecumenic but we have two basic points to keep in mind, viz.:

(a) even in the far distant future architecture should not be influenced only by ecumenic forces, and
(b) it will take us quite a long time to reach the phase in which ecumenic forces will control the architecture of the whole world.

This means that we have to pay attention to the relationship between traditional and contemporary in every instance of architectural creation.

Moreover, we shall have to turn our attention much more to the traditional solutions, for they have a lot to teach us not only about the locality we are working for, but also about the ecumenic architecture which is developing throughout the world. The fact is that we know very little about the experience which has been accumulated by many local civilizations over thousands of years.

Our desire for that which is new, our desire for discovery, has cut the long threads which connected us with our past. Yet this desire for the new is misplaced in many respects. We should not worry so much about new solutions as about right solutions. If the right solutions lead us back to tradition we should not be afraid.

If we now compare the relationship between traditional and new solutions, then we shall see that the percentage of traditional solutions is probably higher than the percentage representing the influence of local forces. This is because almost all the local forces which will prevail in the future are connected with tradition. But in addition to that there are also ecumenic forces, which will be preserved and will play a role in the future, although they are not new but have emerged from the past. In this respect we should be careful in the future to recognize the relationship between the traditional and the new forces. As an example I would like to mention the notion of space and the dimensions of space within buildings (rooms, etc.) and outside them (minor squares, roads for pedestrians, etc.) where the human scale is concerned (Fig. 98).

When contrasting the traditional with the new in the formation of the contemporary we must not imagine that there will be a clear-cut distinction, and that we are going to have areas of traditional solutions and areas of new solutions. On the contrary, we shall witness the emergence of both traditional and new solutions within the same civilization, even within the same urban area, the same locality, even the same project. This will come about because we are creating many types of architectural space for many types of people of different income groups, professional and social classes; moreover it will depend on the degree to which every such class or group of people absorbs the new forces and adopts the new solutions as well as on the level of architectural creation. For example if we are inside an old house, a building, a small street or square, we will then recognize the traditional element, as we have come closer to the factors which have conditioned the traditional solutions. On the contrary, if we reach the size of a metropolis, then location, order of magnitude and formation are the same all over the world. But one metropolis still differs from another in its minor elements and can differ much

Fig. 98. Traditional and new architectural creation

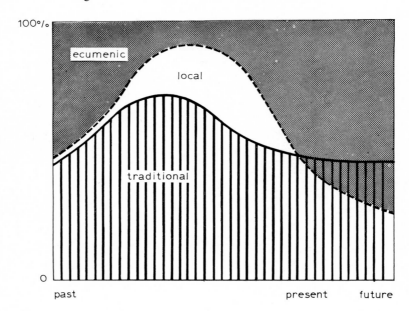

more the farther we move on the micro-scale of the city towards the house. Thus, one metropolis can differ from another in its micro-patterns of land use, free spaces and green, in the formation of the human or minor communities or sectors within it and in the micro-space created within and between houses.

Is this kind of differentiation valuable? I think it is. It serves the people best as it gives them a better solution to a large number of problems which are conditioned by local people and local forces. There is no need to transfer the international contemporary forces to the micro-space of our living if we don't have special reasons for doing so. Certainly, though, if some day this also proves necessary, if some day people will feel happier by having air-conditioning every-where and they can afford to have it, then even this reservation may no longer hold good. But since that is really something in the distant future, and since we must have great reservations about living in an artificial climate, I think we should speak of the need to keep as many of the local traditional forces in play as we can.

But is this in fact possible? The answer is a positive 'yes'. This is because the infiltration of international elements really starts at the outskirts of the city, at the harbour, the airport or the railway station where the internationally conceived machines play the greatest role. These elements infiltrate from there into the main arteries of the city, where cars play the greatest role and into the heart of the city where foreign forces play a certain role. But they do not infiltrate into our private lives very quickly. The external factors really influence a city from the elements of the highest order downwards, whilst the elements of a lower order are not so directly influenced. We may import solutions for a steel bridge, but there is no need for us to do the same for our houses.

Some day, perhaps years or even decades or a century hence, these forces will even have infiltrated as far as every single house. This time lag constitutes the breathing space in which we can try to alter the present trend and create the proper urban frame for our architecture. Such an urban frame will have:

(a) international characteristics in its main elements; and
(b) local-traditional characteristics in its micro-space.

What might these latter be? I think I could mention several. First, the neighbourhood, the small community with internal cohesion and even administrative expression. This we can keep, controlled by the pedestrian, retaining its own character, its own micro-climate, its own micro-society—a micro-community, in fact. We can also keep the human scale where people walk about unimpeded by cars, and we can even create a micro-climate within our cities by appropriate use of gardens, open spaces and water.

In some cases, as in hot climates, we can keep the internal court-yard for the houses, open or covered. This is an element which could survive to the benefit of houses that may even be air-conditioned some day, when air-conditioning is far more economically feasible.

On the other hand, the new forces are by necessity breaking into certain other patterns, such as those of international transportation, of main transportation lines, means of communication, industrial pro-duction, etc. But it would be worse than stupid to allow, without careful consideration, these same forces to break unconditionally the patterns which are of such importance in our lives as the patterns of our houses.

When confronted with this problem of the coexistence of different patterns we must try to see whether such a solution is perhaps only a compromise between new and traditional patterns; if it is, then it can promise only a temporary solution and as such would not have any permanent value. What we need, however, is a solution which would be no meaningless compromise but a *synthesis* of the existing with the new forces, each category of which will operate at a different level. If we can achieve this synthesis, then we shall have made an enormous contribution to the future of architecture. What is more, we shall have rendered a useful service to the people, since such a synthesis would constitute an expression of its own forces. It would also be a service to humanity because, by preserving some of the natural forces of civilization, and by demonstrating this necessity for all areas, we could help lead to a civilization which would become ecumenic not by suppressing the national-local civilizations, but by bringing them into the free synthesis of a single ecumenic civilization.

FROM SUBJECTIVE TO OBJECTIVE

Architecture has until now been based on subjective methods of approach. We usually relate a whole architectural creation to the subjective approach, basing this approach on an enormous amount of subjective information which is itself very often completely misleading.

In dealing with such important questions as that of how we want to live, however, we cannot rely solely on subjective methods of approach. We need a much more objective methodology.

We have already spoken of ekistics as the science of human settlements and of our attempts to develop it, but we must recognize that it is still very young as a science. We have to intensify our search for an objective, scientific approach to all problems related to human settlements and architectural creation. The fact that we are now beginning to understand phenomena such as the dynamic growth of the city—leading to the new concept of dynapolis—should not satisfy us. On the contrary, it should frighten us by showing how much we have overlooked and how long and difficult is the task on which we have embarked.

Thinking of architecture and our methods of approach, we should not overlook the fact that humanity is gradually acquiring the ability to study many phenomena such as economic development and biological evolution, and to proceed to a synthesis as in a modern musical composition in a much more analytical manner. There are two basic reasons for this:

(a) many of these phenomena (for example the economies of countries) are becoming more and more complicated, which makes such analytic study imperative; and
(b) humanity itself is becoming better equipped to discover and investigate the secrets of these phenomena.

In order to reach more objective solutions in architecture we have to carry out proper research. It is only through such research that we can get to the point of understanding the differences between the total architectural activity which is not influenced by the architects, the architectural activity of the architects and the hybrid solutions in between. It is only through such research that we can be sure of finding ways to merge the natural solutions with those given by the architects, so as to eliminate the hybrids and achieve a continuous and consistent effort throughout the spectrum of architectural creation (Fig. 99).

Another advantage we may expect from research is that new theories may help us understand our failures and then arrive at more suitable solutions. One of our great problems in present-day architecture, for example, is the uniformity towards which we are being led by standardization, prefabrication, etc.; a uniformity which is reaching a point at which we can no longer distinguish our own house from our neighbour's. We have reached the point at which it might well be profitable to apply the modern communication theory to the study of such phenomena of uniformity; this may prove to us what variety of messages we should receive from an architectural synthesis in order to satisfy all our needs. This, as well as cybernetics and other new theories, will gradually facilitate our better understanding of the complex problems we are facing.

Yet objective analysis will not provide the final solution to the problems of architectural synthesis, for it is unquestioned that the final solution itself must be subjective. It is very dangerous, how-

Fig. 99.   The spectrum of architectural creation in our time. The infiltration of
architect's architecture into the main body of natural architecture varies and
creates a layer of hybrid solutions

A Architect's architecture

H Hybrid architecture

N Natural architecture

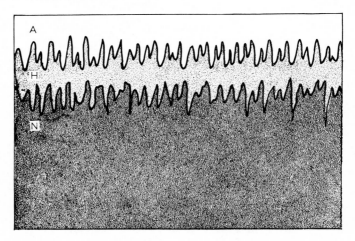

ever, to proceed towards subjective solutions of such complicated
problems with only a subjective analysis of the situation. The proper
method would be to base our thinking on an objective analysis of the
architectural problems, and work out a series of objective solutions;
but we must then proceed to a final solution which should be sub-
jectively related to every specific case for any given problem and for
any given locality. It is the proper balance between objective and subjective methods that is going to make an architecture of the future
worthy of its name. To rely only on subjective solutions will mean a
move backwards, but to rely only on objective solutions will, on the
contrary, mean the end of architectural creation.

FROM UTILITARIAN TO MONUMENTAL

Before closing this discussion, however, it seems necessary to stress
again how dangerous it is that the whole attention of our present era
should be directed towards the non-repeated types of buildings, which
usually tend to become monuments.

People taking this road think that they are simply repeating what has happened in history, from which we only remember the non-repeated monumental buildings. But this is wrong. It is true that those historical buildings were the ones representative of the architectural creation of their time, but that was simply because they were at the top of the cone of the total architectural creation and because our cultures were different.

The proper road is to start from the utilitarian buildings and be concerned only with them, to develop a utilitarian architecture and let it gradually grow into a monumental one. No reasonable effort towards architectural creation in the future can begin unless it is based on utilitarian buildings. They are the buildings that everybody is concerned about, it is to them that the greatest forces of industry, of government and of private individuals should be allocated, and it is at this level that we can create an architecture which may some day find its monumental expression in some few buildings of extra-ordinary importance, if our culture creates a content and a meaning for them.

If monumental buildings will be required by our culture, then, in progressing from utilitarian buildings which are to be repeated towards similar buildings which are not often repeated, almost without being aware of it, we shall in due time find ourselves creating monumental buildings.

In this way we shall move gradually from the commonplace and the temporary towards the exceptional and the lasting; but this cannot take place overnight, within a short period, or even on the basis of a prescribed time-schedule. We must stop our desperate efforts to create a style. If we let architecture develop properly it will almost naturally be led towards a new ecumenic style, the architect of which will be the whole of humanity. When it is created it will no more be possible for a future historian of art to name the architect of the new style than we can today name the architect of the Classical Greek, the Mogul, the Gothic, the Japanese, the Renaissance or of any other great style of humanity.

It is only by thinking in these terms, by getting our role into its proper perspective, that we can justify our present creation and play our proper role as the agents of the human civilization and culture which is developing.

out of the darkness

I AM back again in the dark circus from which I started to grope about, trying to find my way. There are many roads ahead but I am no longer confused. I know now that architecture is passing through a period of transition and that in spite of difficulties we can find a way ahead.

The road we have to take leads towards a human and ecumenic architecture which, instead of eliminating all local expressions, will incorporate them in an architecture which will continue and not set aside the traditions of the past.

Our road is not simply a road of revolution. The previous generation of architects—the great masters and their followers—have done their duty: they started the revolution and established the beachheads. The movement is now losing momentum and in many respects it is tending towards a new academism—the academism of the modern. We cannot remain revolutionaries, but much less may we turn the work of the revolutionaries themselves into a style.

We are at the beginning of a process. Our main task is to consolidate the findings of the revolution, to interconnect the beachheads and carry the movement forward from there.

Personally, after twenty-five years of wandering about the world and working for many peoples, I find I have an obligation to follow only that road ahead of me that is not obstructed and cluttered up with monuments, a road whose largest shadows will be cast by simple, plain, human buildings. In my wanderings around countries and places I have learnt to be able to visit not only other areas but other times too. I have been enabled to turn back the clock of my mind three thousand years in the swamps of Iraq, a thousand years in the delta of Bengal, many thousands of years with the nomads of the desert or mere centuries with the settlers of Australia and America. I have been enabled to see how people live and to understand their problems. I have thus learnt to see the evolution of architecture.

Let me state yet once more my simple creed. I believe that we live in a formative age, an age in which we are to be faced with difficulties and problems in architecture as never before. I can now see that the road ahead of us extends through deserts and rocks, but that it is a road that may lead us into sunlit valleys. We must understand that the solutions we seek are not to be found only in the centres of civilization. They are to be found everywhere, because the roots of this magnificent tree we want to plant and see growing and maturing, will have to draw their nourishment from all parts of a developing humanity.

We need to understand that, like the tree, our architecture is not going to grow overnight. It will take its time and we can only help it grow. We, on our part, must develop the attitude of a gardener who cultivates a tree but does not become anxious and expect fruit before its maturity. We need to understand our proper position in time and not be in a hurry for results. We should not think of forms, but create space, build and live. Architecture will come.

Moreover, we need to understand that the architect cannot survive as a designer of single buildings, much less of monuments, but only as a co-ordinator of architectural activity; in a word, as a master builder. He must be a man able to understand that the forces to be found in a tent in the desert or a hut in the swamps or a factory in the busy hive of industry are sometimes greater than those to be found on the highways of a great metropolis, or in the studio of the architect himself. He must be able to feel himself a mason whose task is to build contemporary buildings and prepare himself for an ecumenic architecture, an architecture which needs to be contemporary and human now in order to become ecumenic in the future.

He must become a scientist, carry out research, create a system of thought, devise a programme of action and carry out proper schemes of organization in government, in industry, in production, in design. He must be a builder.

He must be a man able to work the long day through, bent double under a load of bricks and mortar and stone and steel, laying foundations; but able, when evening falls, to leave his work-site and climb some high rock, there to gaze out to the horizon of a rising world whose dynamic evolution will lead to a dynamic architecture. If the architect is able to be all this, a mason in his work but a dreamer in his ideas, then he may be able to help us found the architecture of a world to come.

In the end, then, this book is more than just a creed: it is an appeal to every architect to act in order to save architecture, an appeal to every one of us to raise his voice for a better human habitat.

As the poet said:

> Become an artisan;
> Connect, attend, concern yourself, enquire . . .
> Wipe out whatever cuts you off;
> Betroth yourself, commit your ring
> To the broad canal of common man;
> Become as one of the countless pillars
> Of the great companionable task.

index

Bold figures indicate illustrations